Option Strategies for Earnings Announcements

Option Strategies for Earnings Announcements

A Comprehensive, Empirical Analysis

Ping Zhou
John Shon

Vice President, Publisher: Tim Moore
Associate Publisher and Director of Marketing: Amy Neidlinger
Executive Editor: Jim Boyd
Editorial Assistant: Pamela Boland
Operations Specialist: Jodi Kemper
Marketing Manager: Megan Graue
Cover Designer: Chuti Prasertsith
Managing Editor: Kristy Hart
Project Editor: Betsy Harris
Copy Editor: Cheri Clark
Proofreader: Leslie Joseph
Senior Indexer: Cheryl Lenser
Compositor: Nonie Ratcliff
Manufacturing Buyer: Dan Uhrig

© 2013 by Ping Zhou and John Shon
Published by Pearson Education, Inc.
Publishing as FT Press
Upper Saddle River, New Jersey 07458

This book is sold with the understanding that neither the author nor the publisher is engaged in rendering legal, accounting, or other professional services or advice by publishing this book. Each individual situation is unique. Thus, if legal or financial advice or other expert assistance is required in a specific situation, the services of a competent professional should be sought to ensure that the situation has been evaluated carefully and appropriately. The author and the publisher disclaim any liability, loss, or risk resulting directly or indirectly, from the use or application of any of the contents of this book.

FT Press offers excellent discounts on this book when ordered in quantity for bulk purchases or special sales. For more information, please contact U.S. Corporate and Government Sales, 1-800-382-3419, corpsales@pearsontechgroup.com. For sales outside the U.S., please contact International Sales at international@pearsoned.com.

Company and product names mentioned herein are the trademarks or registered trademarks of their respective owners.

All rights reserved. No part of this book may be reproduced, in any form or by any means, without permission in writing from the publisher.

Printed in the United States of America

First Printing October 2012

ISBN-10: 0-13-294739-0
ISBN-13: 978-0-13-294739-8

Pearson Education LTD.
Pearson Education Australia PTY, Limited
Pearson Education Singapore, Pte. Ltd.
Pearson Education Asia, Ltd.
Pearson Education Canada, Ltd.
Pearson Educación de Mexico, S.A. de C.V.
Pearson Education—Japan
Pearson Education Malaysia, Pte. Ltd.

Library of Congress Cataloging-in-Publication data is on file.

To Kelly and Rong
—*Ping Zhou*

*To Lucy, whose favorite phrase—
"Let's make money!"—is the inspiration
for this endeavor.*
—*John Shon*

Contents

Preface xv

Part I   Introduction 1

Chapter 1   Earnings Announcements:
             Opportunities and Risks 3
             Earnings Announcements:
             Major, Recurring Events 4
             Market Reactions to Earnings Announcements 4
             Earnings Surprises 7
             Market Reactions to Earnings Surprises Are Full
             of Surprises 8
             Endnotes 9

Chapter 2   Option Strategies for Earnings Announcements:
             An Overview 11
             Why Options? 11
             General Considerations When Designing Option
             Strategies 14
                    Strike Price 14
                    Expiration Date 15
                    Timing of Trades 15
             Classifications of Option Strategies
             for Earnings Announcements 16
             Directional Trades around Earnings Announcements 17
             Volatility Trades around Earnings Announcements 18
                    Longing Volatility 18
                    Shorting Volatility 19
             Volatility Trades before Earnings Announcements 21
             Directional Trades after Earnings Announcements 21

Chapter 3	Liquidity Risk: Bid-Ask Spreads 23
	Measurement of Liquidity: The Bid-Ask Spread...............................24
	Distribution of Absolute and Percentage Bid-Ask Spreads......................................25
	Calls 25
	Puts...29
	The Impact of Different Bid-Ask Spread Assumptions on Performance......................................31
	How Do Bid-Ask Spread Assumptions Impact the Returns of Calls?....................34
	How Do Bid-Ask Spread Assumptions Impact the Returns of Puts?....................35
	The Takeaway 36
	Endnotes 37
	Appendix...37

Part II Option Strategies for Earnings Announcements: Let the Data Speak 39

Chapter 4	Bullish Directional Trades........................41
	Long Calls: The Baseline Case 42
	Short Puts: The Baseline Case 43
	Time Series Analysis 44
	Turning the Dials...................................46
	Out-of-the-Money Options 46
	Further Expiration Dates 48
	Increasing the Holding Period 49
	Thought Experiment: Knowing Earnings Announcement Returns...51
	The Takeaway 55
	Endnotes 56
	Appendix..56
Chapter 5	Bearish Directional Trades 59
	Long Puts: The Baseline Case.........................59
	Short Calls: The Baseline Case 61
	Time Series Analysis 62

	Turning the Dials................................... 63
	Out-of-the-Money Options 64
	Further Expiration Dates 66
	Increasing the Holding Period 67
	Thought Experiment: Knowing Earnings Announcement Returns... 69
	The Takeaway 73
	Endnotes 74
	Appendix... 75
Chapter 6	**Long Volatility Trades** **79**
	Long Straddles: The Baseline Case..................... 80
	Long Strangles: The Baseline Case..................... 82
	Time-Series Analysis 83
	Turning the Dials.................................... 85
	Further Expiration Dates 85
	Increasing the Holding Period 86
	Thought Experiment: Knowing Absolute Earnings Announcement Returns............................. 88
	The Takeaway 90
	Endnote 91
	Appendix... 91
Chapter 7	**Short Volatility Trades** **95**
	Short Straddles: The Baseline Case 96
	Short Strangles: The Baseline Case 97
	Time-Series Analysis 98
	Turning the Dials.................................... 99
	Further Expiration Dates 100
	Increasing the Holding Period 101
	Thought Experiment: Knowing Absolute Earnings Announcement Returns............................. 102
	The Takeaway 105
	Endnote 106
	Appendix... 106

Chapter 8	Buy Volatility before Earnings Announcements........109
	Buying Volatility before Earnings Announcements: The Baseline Case 110
	Time Series Analysis 111
	Turning the Dials................................. 112
	Further Expiration Dates 113
	Increasing the Holding Period (or Entering the Position Earlier)............................. 114
	Thought Experiment: Knowing Absolute Pre-Earnings Announcement Returns........................... 115
	The Takeaway 117
	Endnote 118
	Appendix... 118
Chapter 9	Ride the Post-Earnings-Announcement Drift 121
	Post-Earnings-Announcement Drift in Stock Prices 123
	Options Strategies for Post-Earnings-Announcement Drift 125
	Bullish Directional Trades..................... 126
	Bearish Directional Trades 127
	Time Series Analysis 128
	The Takeaway 130
	Appendix... 131
Part III	**Advanced Analysis: Improve the Odds of Winning** **135**
Chapter 10	Implied Volatility 137
	Implied Volatility and Absolute Earnings Announcement Returns............................. 138
	Implied Volatility and the Performance of Long and Short Straddles around Earnings Announcements 141
	The Evolution of Implied Volatility around Earnings Announcements 144
	The Takeaway 148
	Appendix... 149

Chapter 11	Historical Earnings Announcement Returns 151
	Historical and Future Earnings Announcement Returns... 151
	Historical Absolute Earnings Announcement Returns and the Performance of Long and Short Straddles around Earnings Announcements..................... 156
	The Takeaway 158
	Endnote 159
	Appendix....................................... 159
Chapter 12	Market Capitalization........................... 161
	Market Cap and Absolute Earnings Announcement Returns... 162
	Market Cap and Performance of Long and Short Straddles around Earnings Announcements 165
	The Takeaway 167
	Endnotes 168
	Appendix....................................... 168
Chapter 13	Valuation...................................... 169
	Valuation and Absolute Earnings Announcement Returns... 171
	Valuation and Performance of Long and Short Straddles around Earnings Announcement Returns 174
	The Takeaway 181
	Appendix....................................... 181
Chapter 14	Industry Effects 183
	Industry Classifications 184
	Absolute Earnings Announcement Returns by Sector..... 184
	Implied Volatility by Sector......................... 187
	Performance of Long and Short Straddles around Earnings Announcements by Sector................... 187
	The Takeaway 191
	Endnote 192
	Appendix....................................... 192

Chapter 15	Enhanced Strategies........................195	
	Enhancing the Volatility Strategy:	
	A Two-Factor Model........................196	
	Long Straddles........................196	
	Short Straddles........................198	
	Further Enhancement........................199	
	Historical Absolute Earnings Announcement Returns........................200	
	Valuation........................201	
	Industry Membership........................203	
	The Takeaway........................204	
	Endnotes........................205	
	Index........................207	

Acknowledgments

We thank Jim Boyd for his input and encouragement.

About the Authors

Ping Zhou, Portfolio Manager and Senior Vice President at Neuberger Berman, specializes in portfolio theory, market anomalies, investor behavior, corporate finance, and risk management. Formerly Accounting Professor at City University of New York–Baruch College, he publishes extensively in leading academic and practitioner journals on equity investing. He holds a Ph.D. in Accounting from Georgia State University's Robinson College of Business.

John Shon, Prof. of Accounting at Fordham's Gabelli School of Business and Graduate School of Business Administration, has earned several grants and awards for his equity markets research and has published extensively in academic journals. He holds a Ph.D. in Accounting and an MBA from the University of Chicago's Booth School of Business.

Preface

Do you find yourself intimidated by stock market volatility? If so, you are not alone. Nowadays, more and more investors are intimidated by the volatility that has become the norm. After the crash in 2008, the next three years were characterized by extremely bumpy rides as well. In 2009, you saw your stocks tank by 20% in a little over two months. Just as you completely lost faith in the equity market, one of the most spectacular rallies in history began. In both 2010 and 2011, you enjoyed a strong rally in the first few months of the year, and then, all of a sudden, the market was plagued by deep worries about the European debt crisis and the prospect of global economic recession or worse. Major indices lost 20% and the bears predicted bigger disasters to come. Facing this crisis, central banks started pumping liquidity into the economy. While pundits warned that central banks were going to fail miserably and hyperinflation was just around the corner, the market roared back. In short, it takes a very strong stomach to bear these market swings. Not surprisingly, many are bailing out of stocks and rushing into bonds, despite the fact that bond yields are incredibly low and the prospect of any rise in inflation could easily cause significant damage to bond investors.

You are facing a dilemma: You despise high volatility in the stock market and yet you fear the rich valuation of the bond market. What should you do? One of the solutions is to invest in absolute return strategies that are more or less independent of (the direction of) market movements and the state of the economy. For instance, event-driven strategies design investments around mergers and acquisitions or other specific events and actions. Because the returns of event-driven strategies depend mostly on the outcome of the events targeted, such strategies are relatively neutral to the general market.

This book introduces an event-driven strategy centered on the most salient and regularly recurring corporate event, the quarterly earnings announcement. The trading strategy recommended involves financial derivatives. Not all derivatives are evil and dangerous. In fact, many offer you better risk management and opportunities not available in the cash market. For example, in the stock market you can buy a stock if you are bullish and short it if you are bearish. However, what can you do if you think the market's reaction to an upcoming earnings announcement will be large but you cannot decide which way it will go? You cannot buy the stock and sell it short at the same time, but you can express such a view in the options market by buying call and put options at the same time (i.e., long a straddle or strangle).

Trading opportunities around earnings announcements, including straddles and strangles, were examined at length in our previous book, *Trading on Corporate Earnings News*. However, we did not document the profitability of the strategies using a large population of real trading data. Like many other trading books, we provided examples, but we did not present the results of tests that showed how profitable (or unprofitable) a strategy might be when applied to a broad base of many securities. So this is the first important contribution of this new book. No prior options book has provided this information. We analyze the full universe of all equity options contracts traded over 14 years from 1996 to 2009, examine the data on literally millions of observations (gigs and gigs of data), and report to you the *objective, empirical results.* No more cherry-picking of good results and brushing aside of bad results. We present to you the full distribution of historical returns on option strategies around earnings announcements, so you are fully informed. That is a significant amount of data that you would never have the time (or desire) to pore over yourself. We help you rise above the din, and boil this data down to *powerful information.* In easily understandable tables, we arm you with the knowledge of how various options trades fare on an *empirical basis.*

Have you had the *general sense* that, say, short near-the-money straddles, entered a day before earnings announcements and exited the day after earnings announcements, were a winning play? Well, no more guessing or having a general sense. Our conservative analysis shows that short straddles had a *median* two-day return of 1.93%. That's a significant return for two days. However, the *mean* two-day return was in fact negative, –3.83%. This suggests that well over half of the short straddles were winning plays (given that the median is positive), but that a few large losing trades brought down the average returns, perhaps not surprising given that short options strategies have a fat left tail. But what is this information worth to you—the fact that the median returns are 1.93%, as opposed to some *general sense* of value? There's a huge difference in a positive return of approximately 0.1% versus perhaps 10% versus...exactly 1.93%. And wouldn't you like to know what percentage of all such trades are winners? We know that it's more than 50%. But is it 51% or 80%? (We're not telling you just yet.) Is it enough for you to know that the overall median returns were 1.93%? Or would you like to know how the strategies fared in certain industries and certain years? A short straddle entered in the manufacturing industry in a boring, uneventful year like 2005 is probably different from the same strategy for a financial firm in 2008 and 2009. We document these differences to inform you about how options-based strategies fare in different industries and different years. This precision in information is what we aim to offer the careful reader. It helps arm you with knowledge that enables you to fully understand the odds of your trade being profitable based on real historical data.

The second purpose of this book is our presentation of what-if scenarios. In each chapter, you will find a specific options strategy. Our baseline analysis is always of at-the-money or near-the-money options with the closest expiration date. We also set a standard holding period of two days. Though this baseline analysis is certainly interesting, a natural question that arises is how the distribution of returns would differ if the trades were executed using a different strike price, or a different expiration month. How would the trades differ if we extended the holding period? We answer all of these questions in our extended analysis by presenting each of these alternative what-if scenarios. This enables you to make your own judgment about the types of trades you want to put on, as well as the particular features of trades that you like or don't like, and what is more profitable versus not. These *robustness tests* also further ensure that our baseline results are not some empirical anomaly.

Also, there are several ways of exploiting earnings announcements. For instance, we can consider three general time-related windows around the announcements. The most straightforward is the two-day window capturing the actual announcement. However, we also examine potential trades that occur days or weeks *before* the earnings announcement, to potentially exploit the buildup of implied volatility before the earnings announcement. And we examine separate trades entered *after* the earnings announcement, to potentially exploit possible post-earnings-announcement drift. Each of these three trading windows—before, during, and after the earnings announcement—presents its own features and each deserves separate analysis.

The third feature of this book is that we explore ways to systematically improve the profitability of the general strategies. Put differently, we design a quantitative process to enhance security selection. For example, in stock investing, researchers have long documented that stocks with low price-to-book ratios tend to beat the overall market by a large margin in the long run. Therefore, low price-to-book ratio is a quantifiable characteristic that you might prefer. This book's approach is similar to what other researchers have done for stock investing. We look for quantifiable characteristics that can potentially help you select better candidates for your option strategies. For example, should you buy straddles with higher or lower implied volatility before earnings announcements? Is there information in historical earnings announcement returns? Should you focus on large or small companies? Does the valuation of the company matter? What is the effect of the industry that the company belongs to? These are all important questions which we provide answers to. Armed with such information, you will be able to enhance the returns of your option strategies significantly.

The book is divided into three parts. In Part I (Chapters 1 to 3), we lay down the foundational work by explaining the unique features of earnings announcements, the structure of the analyses, and the important issues related to the liquidity of options, measured by bid-ask spreads. In Part II (Chapters 4 to 9), we present the results of the general strategies including both directional and volatility trades, as well as trades before and after earnings announcements. In Part III (Chapters 10 to 15), we explain and analyze factors that can improve your security selection process. In the final chapter (Chapter 15), we present enhanced strategies that exploit each of these factors simultaneously.

Part I
Introduction

In this section, we introduce the philosophy behind our main trading strategies. We specifically discuss three important questions that motivate our investigation. Why do we focus on earnings announcements? What options strategies are available to explore different aspects of earnings announcements? What is the impact of liquidity on the performance of option-based trading strategies?

In Chapter 1, we discuss the most important features of quarterly earnings announcements and document large market reactions to them. Such volatile price movements present excellent trading opportunities, but directional bets on earnings announcements can be highly risky. In Chapter 2, we go over some of the basics of options trading and provide an overview of the options strategies for earnings announcements. The strategies are grouped along two lines: timing and rationale. Chapter 3 examines a critical yet often ignored aspect of options trading: liquidity, measured by the bid-ask spread. We show that different assumptions of the bid-ask spread (at what prices trades are entered and unwound) have a significant impact on a strategy's profitability, and we strongly propose a conservative approach in considering bid-ask spreads in live trading.

1

Earnings Announcements: Opportunities and Risks

In today's topsy-turvy investing environment, a crisis (real or imagined) is always just around the corner. Just as we're licking our wounds from a prior crisis, there is a larger one looming on the horizon. How do you navigate through this turmoil? We propose *event-driven trading*—because in many ways it steers clear of general market movements and can even strive in them. Our favorite type of event is the quarterly earnings announcement. Because earnings announcement trades involve transacting around a short, well-defined window of time, they can, when properly implemented, produce positive returns regardless of the market environment. (They're almost market neutral in this respect.) In this chapter, you'll discover why trading around earnings announcements has potential, and what features these trades possess that make them more desirable candidates for options trading than other events (like, for example, dividend change announcements). Do earnings announcements garner a sufficient market reaction to be worthy of event-driven trading? What are earnings surprises? More importantly, do the market reactions "match up" (in direction and magnitude) to these earnings surprises? How can options-based trades complement the features of these earnings-related events? These are some of the questions we answer in this chapter.

Earnings Announcements: Major, Recurring Events

Corporations make many public disclosures during any given year. Mergers and acquisitions, change of board directors, insiders' trading of stock, and dividend announcements are all examples. However, most of the disclosures are not recurring and their timing is hard to estimate. Moreover, the impact of most disclosures on share prices is small or nonexistent. The type of disclosures that are desirable for an event-driven investor are recurring, have a predictable schedule, and have a potentially sizable impact on share prices. A disclosure that meets all these requirements is the quarterly earnings announcement.

The Securities and Exchange Commission (SEC) requires all publicly traded companies to file quarterly 10-Q financial reports. Most companies announce their quarterly performance a few weeks before the 10-Q is filed with the SEC. These quarterly announcements are typically referred to as the firm's *earnings announcements* because earnings per share (EPS) is *the* number contained in the announcement that everyone is most paying attention to. These regularly recurring earnings announcements are by far the most salient, most anticipated, and most reliable news that companies publish. It is the most-watched piece of information that comes directly "from the source"—the company itself. It's no wonder that these earnings announcements move prices.

Market Reactions to Earnings Announcements

How large an impact do earnings announcements have on share prices? We have studied this question by analyzing all the quarterly earnings announcements of the largest 1,000 stocks (measured by market capitalization) during the 1984–2009 period. We measured earnings announcement returns over a three-day window that spanned from the day before earnings announcement to the day after. We examined 110,495 *market-adjusted* (excess) returns to earnings announcements made by Russell 1000 firms during the 1984–2009 period. Table 1.1 shows the distribution of (market-adjusted) stock market reactions to these earnings announcements.[1] Overall, for all the earnings announcement returns spanning the full 26 years, the median announcement return was 10 basis points for the three-day window—about zero. This suggests that there were about as many positive earnings announcement returns as there were negative ones. Next, we looked at the average (mean) announcement return (presented in the bottom row). Coming in at 20 basis points for the three-day window returns, we concluded that, on *average,* earnings announcement returns were not that large at all. However, it would be a huge mistake to conclude from these numbers that the market reactions to earnings announcements were always small. After all, the average is just that: an average. It doesn't tell us much about the variation in the returns.

Table 1.1 Distribution of Earnings-Announcement Excess Returns of Russell 1000 Stocks from 1984 to 2009

Distribution	3-Day Window Return
Maximum	246.24%
90th Percentile	17.41%
75th Percentile	2.74%
50th Percentile (Median)	0.10%
25th Percentile	−2.34%
10th Percentile	−5.59%
Minimum	−84.24%
Mean	0.20%

To examine the variation in returns, consider the quartile cutoffs. Specifically, for the three-day window, the 75th percentile excess return was 2.74%, and the 25th percentile excess return was

−2.34%. That means that 25% of the earnings announcements had excess returns greater than 2.74%, and similarly, 25% of the earnings announcements had excess returns more negative than −2.34%. These returns are quite large when compared to the expected returns during a typical three-day period where no earnings were announced. For instance, assume that over the past 50 years, the average return of a random stock was about 7% a year and its annual volatility was about 20%. There are roughly 250 trading days per year, so the mean of daily market returns is about 2.8 basis points (=0.07/250),[2] which means that a typical three-day return is about 8.4 basis points. The volatility over any three-day window is 2.20%. So 50% of the three-day earnings announcement returns (those above the 75th percentile and below the 25th percentile) are more than one standard deviation away from the mean. Assuming a normal distribution, this should happen about 32% of the time, but during earnings announcements it happens more than 50% of the time.[3] If we examine the announcement returns in the 90th and 10th percentiles, the size of the returns is obviously even more significant. The basic message is that market movements during earnings announcement periods are quite large when compared to returns during nonevent periods, and hence offer great opportunities for trading.

When we dig deeper and consider the returns from each individual year between 1984 and 2009, we find an *increasing trend* in the percentile returns over the period. For instance, the 90th percentile announcement-period returns started out at a hair less than 5.0% in 1984, but steadily increased to approximately 12% in 2009. Similarly, the 25th percentile started in 1984 at approximately −2.5%, but ended at about −4.5% in 2009. Even if we ignore years with elevated market volatility (e.g., 2000, 2001, 2008, and 2009), the conclusion is the same: Market reactions to earnings announcements have increased in size and intensity over time. This suggests that the opportunities to profit from options-based trades around earnings announcements have not diminished over the years.

Earnings Surprises

Earnings announcements often convey *earnings surprises*. An earnings surprise is the difference between the actual earnings number reported by a company's management and the market's expectations of what the actual number was going to be. A positive surprise means that the actual earnings are higher than expectations, and a negative surprise means the opposite.[4]

An earnings surprise is typically informative, *new* news (as opposed to useless, stale information, which is not an obvious point, given the 24/7 news cycle). Because of this, earnings announcements are usually met with significant price reactions when the news is released. We analyzed 82,507 earnings surprises during the 1984–2009 sample period.[5] Our analysis revealed that on average the quarterly earnings surprise was –7.49%, but the median earnings surprise was 0.69%. This suggests that more than half the earnings surprises are positive, but there are some very large negative surprises. The 75th percentile earnings surprise was 9.43% (so the top 25% of all earnings surprises were larger than 9.43%) and the 25th percentile earnings surprise was –4.41% (the bottom 25% of all earnings surprises were more negative than –4.41%). These results suggest that a significant number of earnings surprises spanning the last 26 years have been quite large. Imagine how the market reacts when it expects $1.00 of EPS but is greeted with an announcement that actual earnings were $1.09 or $0.96. Over the years 1984–2009, there was a steady decline of negative earnings surprises and a steady increase of positive earnings surprises. More important, the number of zero surprises declined sharply in the past decade. This means that despite the abundance of information in today's non-stop news cycle, earnings surprises seem to be even more common now than they were ten years ago.

Market Reactions to Earnings Surprises Are Full of Surprises

The market tends to react positively to positive earnings surprises and negatively to negative earnings surprises. However, this is not always the case; in fact, *almost 40%* of all positive earnings surprises were met with *negative* excess market reactions on the order of –2%. There were 10% of positive earnings surprises that had returns of –5% or worse. A similar outcome was found for negative earnings surprises. Ten percent of all negative earnings surprises were clocking +4% excess returns. At the 10th and 90th percentiles, even the announcements where companies are "just meeting expectations" (the zero earnings surprise group) were met with close to 6% *absolute* excess market reactions. Thus, for a significant portion of the population, an earnings surprise is going to be met with a market reaction going in the opposite direction of the surprise. Table 1.2 makes this clear. Specifically, over the three-day window, 39.45% of positive earnings surprises had negative stock returns, and 38.95% of the negative earnings surprises had positive stock returns.

Table 1.2 Proportion of Positive and Negative Excess Returns for Positive, Zero, and Negative Earnings Surprises

	3-Day Window Return	
	Positive Excess Return (≥ 0)	*Negative Excess Return (<0)*
Positive Earnings Surprise	60.55%	**39.45%**
Zero Earnings Surprise	48.46%	51.54%
Negative Earnings Surprise	**38.95%**	61.05%

This finding implies that even if you are very skilled in forecasting earnings surprises, you can still incur significant trading losses because the market reactions to these surprises so often go in the opposite direction. There is no evidence that this opposite-reaction phenomenon is diminishing over time. In fact, there is a case to be made that market reactions overall are becoming *more* severe, not less.

Why do so many earnings surprises have returns in the opposite direction? There are many possible reasons to explain this surprising result, but two reasons stand out. First, the content of an earnings announcement includes many other pieces of value-relevant information besides the earnings number itself. Earnings announcement returns reflect the market's reactions to all such information rather than earnings surprises alone. For example, managers might provide their general outlook for the business and specific sales and earnings guidance for the next quarter. If the guidance falls short of the market's expectations, a positive earnings surprise could be overwhelmed by the negative influence of the lowered guidance (or vice versa). Second, it's possible that the earnings surprises calculated in studies such as ours are not the "true" earnings surprises, because there are all kinds of issues in measuring the market's actual expectations. That is, these measures are proxies for an underlying consensus number that no one actually knows for certain.

Predicting the direction of earnings surprises is a very difficult task. Moreover, even if the earnings surprises were perfectly predicted, the *market's reactions* to these surprises can go in the opposite direction. This empirical regularity has important implications for how you can exploit potential trading strategies around earnings announcements.

Endnotes

1. The returns we report are *market-adjusted* or *excess* returns, meaning that we subtracted the corresponding (value-weighted) market returns from each company's raw returns. This adjustment is used to remove the impact of general market movements and to better isolate the returns that the specific

company was experiencing above and beyond general market movements and returns. For instance, if the return during the earnings announcement period for Apple was 3%, but the return for the S&P 500 during the same period was also 3%, then you would have a difficult time saying that Apple had a very good announcement period return since it had the same return that any average company had on that day.

2. The geometric mean, or compounded rate of return, would be even smaller.

3. The caveat of this analysis is that perhaps stocks with large earnings announcement returns tend to be more volatile in general, so the earnings announcement returns we observe are not much different from their nonevent returns. It is certainly true that there is a positive association between a stock's volatility and the magnitude of its earnings announcement return, but there is plenty of evidence showing that absolute stock returns are significantly higher during earnings announcements than in normal days.

4. As obvious and straightforward as this might sound, there are actually several important details about how to define and measure earnings surprises. We provided a detailed discussion of this topic in our first book, *Trading on Corporate Earnings News*.

5. We use analysts' consensus EPS estimate as the market's expectation. To ensure that earnings surprises are comparable across different stocks, we scaled the earnings surprises by the consensus forecasts.

2

Option Strategies for Earnings Announcements: An Overview

Earnings announcements often trigger large market reactions, which is ideal for many types of short-term trades. Moreover, detectable patterns in options' implied volatility and stock prices before and after earnings announcements suggest further trading opportunities. This chapter discusses the advantages of trading options instead of cash stocks around earnings announcements, reviews the basics of options trading, and introduces option strategies designed to exploit several aspects of earnings announcements.

Why Options?

When faced with the opportunity to make a trade based on earnings news, why should you consider using options instead of plain vanilla stocks? After all, many investors would not touch anything involving derivatives with a ten-foot pole.

If you subscribe to the view that options, or any financial derivatives, are evil and dangerous, we invite you to reconsider your view, especially if you want to trade on earnings news. There are three main reasons why adding options to your toolkit is helpful. First, options provide leverage not available to most retail stock investors. For example, Apple (NASDAQ: AAPL) announced its Q1 2012 earnings on January 24, 2012, after hours. The stock closed at around $420. Suppose you were bullish on Apple's earnings news and wanted to buy 100 shares.

The investment required $42,000 of cash, not a small number to many investors. However, you could turn to the options market and buy one contract (which is equivalent to 100 shares) of the March 2012 option with a $420 strike for $1,900 or 4.5% of the capital required for the purchase of 100 shares. If the earnings news were good (they were; Apple's shares jumped 5% the day after the announcement), the call option's value would rise substantially. The call option's total profit in dollars would be less than that of 100 equity shares, however, because the call option's delta is less than one. Nevertheless, the return on investment would be much higher for the option than for the stock investment. This is, of course, the effect of leverage, which has similarly pronounced effects if the trade moves against you.

The second reason why options are useful for trading earnings news is that they offer better risk management in the event that earnings news moves prices against your position. This is because options have an asymmetric payoff function. Specifically, the upside of a call option is theoretically unlimited, but the downside is capped by the premium paid. Recall that the market reactions to earnings surprises are often very large. It is not uncommon for a stock to lose 20% of its value in one day if the company's earnings news misses investors' expectations. With the Apple example, assume you have $42,000 cash and can either buy 100 shares of Apple outright or buy one March 2012 $420 call for $1,900. Suppose the earnings news was bad and investors dumped the shares. If the stock dropped 10% the next day, the stock position would lose $4,200, whereas the option position's maximum loss would be just $1,900. Thus, by using options instead of stocks, you can better protect your downside if the earnings news is *sufficiently* bad ("sufficiently" is the key word here, and we will revisit it in future chapters). It would be disingenuous to address only the better downside protection of the call without talking about the sacrifice of upside potential. If the stock went up 10%, for example, the stock investment would make a $4,200 profit, but the call option would make only around $2,800 (give or take $200). However, if the stock went up 100% (unlikely but possible), the dollar return from the call would be the same as that from the stock investment because the call would be deep in the money after the sharp rise in share price. In short, the gap between the dollar return from the option and the stock investment diminishes as the stock price rises, but the dollar loss from the cash investment exceeds that from the call option at an accelerated speed as the stock price goes down.

The third and most important reason to use options is that they allow you to trade earnings announcements in ways that are not possible with cash securities. This statement relates to volatility trades. For example, if you are convinced that the earnings announcement will trigger a large price reaction but unsure which direction the stock will go, you cannot express this view using equity securities. However, you can express this view by buying both call and put options (that is, longing a straddle/strangle). If the price movement is sufficiently large, the profit from one leg of the trade will exceed the loss from the other leg and result in a net profit. Moreover, there are detectable patterns in the changes of implied volatility before and after earnings announcements that offer trading opportunities. Implied volatility tends to increase leading up to the earnings announcement and then tends to collapse after the announcement. This means that investors are anxious about the earnings news, so they are willing to pay a higher premium for both calls and puts during the time leading up to the earnings announcements. The announcements remove much of the uncertainty, and hence, the implied volatility typically comes down after the announcement. Straddles and strangles, which involve buying or shorting calls and puts at the same time, allow you to profit from volatility changes before and after earnings announcements without having to predict whether the earnings announcement return is positive or negative. Instead, the focus is shifted to predict whether the market reactions to earnings news will be large or small, regardless of the direction, and whether the implied volatility priced into the options will be sufficient to generate a net profit.

General Considerations When Designing Option Strategies

To design option strategies, you will need to set a few parameters and think through the implications of your decision. Your selection criteria for specific features of options determine overall risk and potential reward. These parameters include the option's strike price, expiration date, as well as the specific timing of trades.

Strike Price

An option's strike price can be in-the-money (ITM), at-the-money (ATM), or out-of-the-money (OTM). For instance, for a stock trading at $50, an ATM call would have a strike price of $50. An ITM call would have a strike price of $45 or $40 or lower. And an OTM call would have a strike price of $55 or $60 or higher. We focus on ATM and (slightly) OTM strike prices. In reality, it is rare to have a strike price that exactly matches the underlying stock price—how often is a stock trading at *exactly* $50.00? So ATM is a relative term. We refer to the closest strike price less than 5% away from the stock's traded price as the ATM strike; it is therefore the nearest to ATM, or simply near-the-money (NTM). For instance, if the stock is trading at $51, we would consider the $50 strike price to be ATM or NTM. Similarly, for OTM options, we require the option's strike price to be between 5% and 10% away from the underlying equity's price. We deliberately limit our analysis to this 10% cap. This ignores several options contracts further out of the money. For instance, for the stock that is trading at $51, we would consider the $55 strike as the OTM option (because 10% of $51 is $5.10, and the $55 strike is within this boundary). However, we ignore further-out strikes of $60 or $70 because they are more than 10% away from the underlying stock's price. We ignore these further-out strike prices in our analysis mainly due to concerns about the lack of liquidity. The open interest on further OTM strike prices is lower, as is trading volume. Such thinly traded options are much more difficult to analyze and make general conclusions about because their prices are largely driven by a small number of trades; the noise in pricing can be extremely large, making for volatile trades. And, as we will discuss in the next chapter, it can cause huge differences in the bid and ask spread, making trading profits elusive. For these reasons, we analyze only two strike prices for each underlying stock: the ATM or NTM option (defined as being no more than 5% away from the underlying stock's price) and one OTM option (limited to being no more than 10% away from the stock's price).

Expiration Date

For a given stock and strike price, there are also many expiration dates. For instance, in the preceding example, when a stock is trading at $51, and we choose a NTM strike of $50, we must then choose among several expiration dates. Assume that the current date is July 14. For the $50 strike price, there is a July 20 expiration date, which is only six days away. There are also expiration dates for August, September, October, January and April of next year, and even January of the following year (which is about 18 months away). In our analysis, we limit our examination to the nearest expiration date, and require the expiration to be no more than three months from the earnings announcement month. As with the strike price discussion, we do this mainly because of liquidity concerns: In general, the open interest and trading volume of further expiration dates are lower, making pricing less efficient.

Timing of Trades

Deciding the exact timing of when to enter a trade is critical to the success of the strategies discussed in this book. Some strategies are best implemented right before or after earnings announcements, whereas others need more time to work out so the trades are entered days or even weeks before earnings announcements. The optimal solution to the timing question is jointly determined by the changes in volatility and time decay. We discuss in detail the timing choice of various strategies in the next section.

Classifications of Option Strategies for Earnings Announcements

We analyze various options strategies that target different opportunities associated with earnings announcements. We classify these strategies along two lines.

The first line is the rationale behind the strategy. Here, we categorize each strategy as either a directional trade or a volatility trade. Directional trades aim to profit by predicting the direction of the stock price movement. For example, buying a call ahead of an earnings announcement is a directional trade because the trade tends to profit if the stock price moves up after the earnings announcement and loses money if the stock price moves down. Volatility trades, on the other hand, emphasize the *magnitude* of price movement and the change in implied volatility. The success of volatility trades does not rely on the direction of the actual price movement. For example, buying both calls and puts (i.e., longing a straddle/strangle) ahead of an earnings announcement is a volatility trade because it makes money if the price reaction to earnings news is larger than what is implied by the (combination of both) option prices, regardless of the direction of the price movement.

The second line is the timing. We have strategies designed for pre-, around-, and post-earnings announcements, which are examined in later chapters. The focus of our analysis is on strategies directly surrounding the earnings announcements themselves.

Table 2.1 demonstrates the categorization of the strategies and specifies the chapters in which they are analyzed.

Table 2.1 Categories of Options Strategies for Earnings Announcements

Timing	Rationale	
	Directional	*Volatility*
Before Announcements		Chapter 8
During Announcements	Chapters 4 and 5	Chapters 6 and 7
After Announcements	Chapter 9	

Directional Trades around Earnings Announcements

Directional trades reflect a directional view on the earnings announcement return. The simplest form of directional trades is outright purchases of calls and puts ahead of earnings announcements. The other choice is to short calls or puts.

We classify directional trades as either bullish or bearish trades. Buying a call is a bullish move related to earnings news, whereas buying a put reflects a bearish view. This sounds simple enough, but unfortunately option prices don't always move in line with stock prices—even if the announcement returns are positive, buying a call can still be a money-losing venture. Similarly, buying a put ahead of negative earnings announcement returns can generate a loss. The main reason for this seemingly counterintuitive phenomenon is the volatility collapse that occurs after earnings announcements (because the uncertainty about the earnings news has been resolved). To a lesser degree, time decay works against option buyers too. Therefore, for call or put buying ahead of earnings news to be profitable, not only must the prediction of the direction of the earnings surprise be correct, but the magnitude of the market's reaction to the news must be sufficiently large as well. How large is sufficiently large? It depends on the implied volatility.

The alternative to longing puts and calls is to short them. You can short puts to reflect a bullish view on earnings news. Or, if you expect a negative earnings announcement return, you can short calls. Shorting has the tail winds of volatility collapse and time decay working in your favor, but it also has larger risks. If your prediction of the direction of earnings news is wrong, the losses could be devastating. For this strategy to be profitable, you hope that either your prediction of earnings news is correct or, if your prediction is wrong, that the stock price does not move drastically against you (because volatility collapse and time decay can help soften the blow of small price movements). In Chapter 4, "Bullish Directional Trades," we analyze and compare the performance of buying calls and shorting puts. In Chapter 5, "Bearish Directional Trades," we perform the same analysis on buying puts and shorting calls.

Volatility Trades around Earnings Announcements

Longing Volatility

Earnings announcement returns are very difficult to forecast. Not only do the differences between actual earnings and the market's expectations (that is, earnings surprises) play an important role in determining earnings announcement returns, but other factors, such as revenue surprises and management's outlook, are also influential. Quite often a positive earnings surprise is met with negative earnings announcement return because the revenue fails to meet the market's expectations. And the opposite is also true: Negative earnings surprises are often met by positive stock price reactions. Even when the earnings surprise and revenue surprise agree, management may provide an outlook of the company's future that is inconsistent with these accounting-based surprises, making the market second-guess the information in the earnings and revenue surprises. Therefore, it is challenging to predict the direction of the earnings announcement return. On top of that, even if you correctly predict the direction of the earnings announcement return, the magnitude of the return has to be sufficiently large for directional long option trades to be profitable. All these difficulties suggest that directional trades are risky. The odds of winning may be higher if you need to forecast only the magnitude rather than both the magnitude *and* the direction of earnings announcement returns. Volatility trades allow you to achieve precisely this.

Straddles and strangles are basic volatility trades. They are often referred to as "combination" trades because they involve a combination of both calls and puts. A long straddle means simultaneously buying a call and a put with the same strike price and expiration date. A strangle is similar to a straddle except that the strike price of the call is different from that of the put. In the context of earnings announcements, the natural strike price is the ATM/NTM strike. A long straddle is suitable when you expect the stock to make a big move but you are unsure about the direction of this big move. Earnings announcements fit this description almost perfectly: The release of earnings news often triggers a very large price movement, but it is difficult to predict the direction of the movement. In addition, a long straddle is psychologically appealing because its maximum loss is the total premium paid but its upside is unlimited. Many traders advocate entering a long straddle prior to earnings announcements.

Shorting Volatility

Several factors work against the long volatility strategy. First, not all earnings announcement returns are large in absolute terms. Small earnings announcement returns could be the result of either highly predictable businesses or constant communication between management and financial analysts. In fact, some companies regularly issue earnings forecasts and make other types of public disclosures to help soften the blow of anything too jolting in an imminent earnings announcement. Thus, by the time the actual earnings are announced, there is sometimes not much that the investment community does not already know. Second, option sellers know that earnings announcement returns can be large, so options tend to be more expensive before earnings announcements. For a long straddle strategy to be profitable, not only must the stock have a big move, but the move must be bigger than what is reflected in the option prices. Finally, the volatility collapse that occurs after earnings announcements and the time decay that occurs while holding a long position both work against a long volatility trade as well.

The flip side of a long volatility trade is a short volatility trade, selling short a call and put simultaneously. A short volatility trade is profitable when the stock moves less than implied by the option prices. For example, if the announced earnings are less newsworthy than what the market expected, a short straddle/strangle position will be profitable. The payoff structure of a short straddle/strangle is the opposite of that of the long straddle/strangle: Its maximum gain is the premiums collected but its downside is theoretically unlimited. Because of this psychologically unappealing payoff function, a short volatility trade is considered a highly risky strategy. However, higher option prices prior to announcements, the volatility collapse after the announcements, and the time decay are all tail winds to a profitable short volatility strategy. The risk to this strategy is the tail risk that the market significantly underestimates the magnitude of the earnings announcement return.

In Chapter 6, "Long Volatility Trades," and Chapter 7, "Short Volatility Trades," we analyze long and short volatility strategies. Using tens of thousands of actual earnings announcements spanning 14 years, we systematically answer the questions many investors have on their minds: Is there a systematic way to profit from earnings announcement returns? Is a long straddle better than a short straddle when trading an earnings announcement?

Volatility Trades before Earnings Announcements

Implied volatility tends to increase in the weeks before earnings announcements and reach its peak a day or two before. This is because investors grow more and more anxious about earnings news as the date of earnings announcement approaches. To explore this run-up in volatility, you can enter a long straddle or strangle position prior to earnings announcements and exit the position one or two days before the actual announcements. The success of the strategy depends on several factors, including security selection, timing of the trade, and selection of options. In Chapter 8, "Buy Volatility before Earnings Announcements," we analyze these issues in detail.

Directional Trades after Earnings Announcements

A well-documented phenomenon is the post-earnings-announcement drift (PEAD). Stocks with very positive earnings announcement returns tend to continue their climb upwards (relative to the market) for months after the announcement, and the opposite is true for those with very negative earnings announcement returns. PEAD predicts the direction of a stock's future return, so the option strategy exploiting PEAD is directional in nature. Its implementation is similar to the directional trades around earnings announcements, but it requires trading options with further expiration dates. Chapter 9, "Ride the Post-Earnings-Announcement Drift," examines the design, implementation, and performance of this strategy.

3

Liquidity Risk: Bid-Ask Spreads

Liquidity refers to the ease of entering and exiting a position. It is determined by two factors: trading volume and the bid-ask spread. The two factors are related. Most of the time, when trading volume is high, bid-ask spreads tend to be narrow, and vice versa. For most retail investors, the trading volume of options is not an important constraint (though it can be a significant constraint for large institutional investors). Thus, we focus on the bid-ask spread as the main measure of liquidity in this chapter. We argue that bid-ask spreads in the options market can significantly alter the profitability of strategies. This is because bid-ask spreads in the options market are often prohibitively large when compared to those in the stock market. The issue of bid-ask spreads is not simply a "technical" point reserved for a select few curious investors. It concerns prices paid for buying and selling, so this analysis is crucial and significant in increasing your odds of executing profitable trades. In this chapter, we discuss the measurement of the bid-ask spread, show its empirical distribution, and demonstrate why the results of any strategies making easy assumptions on bid-ask spreads should be interpreted with caution.

Measurement of Liquidity: The Bid-Ask Spread

There are two main approaches to measuring the bid-ask spread. The first approach looks at the absolute difference between the bid and the ask prices, or the "Absolute Bid-Ask Spread." The formula for this measure is the following:

$$\text{Absolute Bid-Ask Spread} = \text{Ask} - \text{Bid}$$

For example, suppose that the bid and ask prices for a call are $1.10 and $1.20. The Absolute Bid-Ask Spread for this call is $0.10 ($1.20 − $1.10). A distinct feature of this measure is that it pays no attention to the *level* of the bid and ask prices. The Absolute Bid-Ask Spread is $0.10 whether the bid and ask are $1.10 and $1.20 or $10.10 and $10.20. Since the trading cost of options is determined by the number of contracts rather than the prices of the options, this measure makes sense from a transaction-cost perspective.

The second approach takes into account the level of the bid and ask prices, and measures the bid-ask spread as a percentage of the midpoint of the bid-ask spread itself. This is the "Percentage Bid-Ask Spread." Its formula is the following:

$$\text{Percentage Bid-Ask Spread} = (\text{Ask} - \text{Bid}) / [(\text{Ask} + \text{Bid}) / 2]$$

When the bid and ask are $1.10 and $1.20 respectively, the Percentage Bid-Ask Spread is 8.70%. However, the Percentage Bid-Ask Spread drops to 0.99% if the bid and ask are $10.10 and $10.20 instead.

The difference between the two measures is significant. From an investment-return perspective, the Percentage Bid-Ask Spread is much more important than the Absolute Bid-Ask Spread. Before we discuss the impact of the bid-ask spread on investment returns in detail, let's first examine the distribution of the two bid-ask spread measures.

Distribution of Absolute and Percentage Bid-Ask Spreads

Our sample starts with all options available from 1996 to 2009. We focus on the ATM calls and puts on the day before earnings announcements. We apply the following rules to finalize the sample:

- We exclude any contracts whose expiration dates are more than three months away from the earnings announcement month. This screen leaves us with the most liquid option contracts.

- The contracts selected for the analysis are the closest contracts with which the ATM/NTM strike price is available. As discussed in Chapter 2, "Option Strategies for Earnings Announcements: An Overview," we define ATM/NTM strike price as the closest price that is within 5% of the underlying stock price.

- We require the minimum bid price of a contract to be $0.30. Approximately 10% of the contracts do not meet this requirement. We impose this requirement because we assume a 3-cent round-trip transaction cost (i.e., commission) for each share,[1] representing 10% of the minimum bid price requirement.

The final sample has 58,666 calls and 58,710 puts.

Calls

Table 3.1 lists the distribution of Absolute Bid-Ask Spreads and Percentage Bid-Ask Spreads for the calls. The mean (median) Absolute Bid-Ask Spread is $0.25 ($0.20), and the mean (median) Percentage Bid-Ask Spread is 17.98% (14.29%). Although the Absolute Bid-Ask Spread seems to be a small number, it represents a large percentage of the midpoint of the bid/ask. What this means is that the option price, measured by the midpoint of the bid/ask, has to go up 17.98% on average if you buy at the ask and sell at the bid to break even.[2] This bid-ask spread head wind is very strong: 90% of the time the midpoint option price must increase at least 5.41% for you to break even if you submit a market order.

Table 3.1 Absolute and Percentage Bid-Ask Spread of Calls

	Absolute Bid-Ask Spread	Percentage Bid-Ask Spread
Mean	$0.25	17.98%
Minimum	$0.01	0.40%
10th Percentile	$0.10	5.41%
25th Percentile	$0.15	8.70%
Median	$0.20	14.29%
75th Percentile	$0.25	22.22%
90th Percentile	$0.38	35.29%
Maximum	$8.30	176.92%

We now analyze what affects the Percentage Bid-Ask Spread. Recall that Percentage Bid-Ask Spread = (Ask − Bid) / [(Ask + Bid) /2]. After simple manipulation, the formula becomes:

Percentage Bid-Ask Spread = 1 / [(Bid / Absolute Bid-Ask Spread) + 1/2]

Examining the denominator, a large Percentage Bid-Ask Spread can be the result of high Absolute Bid-Ask Spread, low Bid-Price, or both. Which factor is the most important?

Table 3.2 shows the mean and median Absolute Bid-Ask Spread and Percentage Bid-Ask Spread for ten equal-sized decile portfolios sorted by the bid price of the calls. From Decile 1 (lowest bid price) to Decile 10 (highest bid price), both the mean and median bid prices of the calls increase monotonically, as expected. Decile 1 has a mean (median) bid price of $0.41 ($0.40), whereas Decile 10 has a mean (median) bid price of $5.08 ($4.00). Roughly speaking, the bid price of Decile 10 is more than 10 times that of Decile 1.

Table 3.2 Absolute and Percentage Bid-Ask Spread, by Call Bid-Price Deciles

Decile	Bid-Price		Absolute Bid-Ask Spread		Percentage Bid-Ask Spread	
	Mean	Median	Mean	Median	Mean	Median
1	0.41	0.40	0.21	0.20	0.39	0.40
2	0.61	0.60	0.21	0.20	0.28	0.29
3	0.79	0.80	0.21	0.20	0.23	0.22
4	0.98	1.00	0.22	0.20	0.19	0.18
5	1.19	1.20	0.22	0.20	0.16	0.15
6	1.44	1.44	0.22	0.20	0.14	0.13
7	1.73	1.75	0.22	0.20	0.12	0.11
8	2.10	2.10	0.27	0.25	0.12	0.11
9	2.70	2.69	0.30	0.25	0.10	0.10
10	5.08	4.00	0.41	0.38	0.08	0.07

But what is the difference in Absolute Bid-Ask Spread between them? The mean (median) Absolute Bid-Ask Spread for Decile 1 is $0.21 ($0.20), whereas that for Decile 10 is $0.41 ($0.38), or roughly twice that of Decile 1. The difference in Absolute Bid-Ask Spread between Decile 1 and Decile 10 is much smaller than their difference in the bid prices. In fact, the Absolute Bid-Ask Spread is quite similar for about 70% of the options (Decile 1 to Decile 7), even though the average bid price has gone up more than five times. These results suggest that the Absolute Bid-Ask Spread is highly sticky, implying that in percentage terms, *the bid-ask spread becomes a smaller issue as the bid price rises*. Indeed, the mean (median) Percentage Bid-Ask Spread drops from 39% (40%) for Decile 1 to 8% (7%) for Decile 10. Figure 3.1 demonstrates the negative correlation between the Absolute Bid-Ask Spread and the Percentage Bid-Ask Spread.

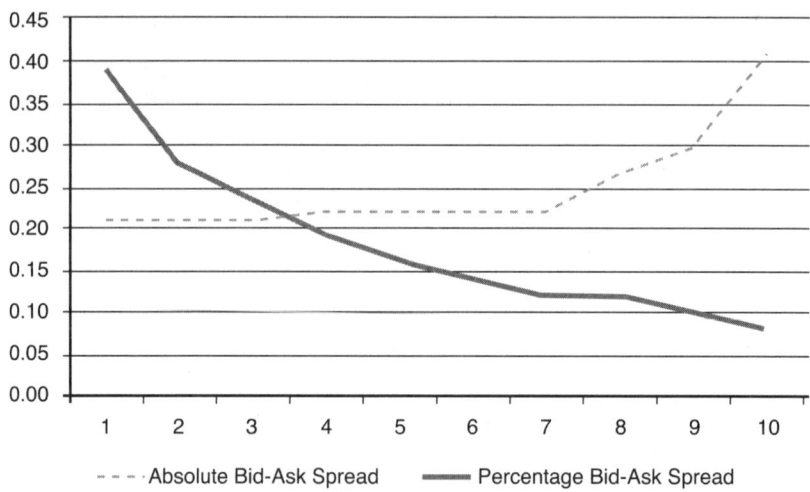

Figure 3.1 Mean Absolute and Percentage Bid-Ask Spread, by Call Bid-Price deciles.

The bid-ask spread can have a significant impact on investment performance, especially for options with relatively small bid prices. For example, let's take an average option in Decile 1 with the $0.40/$0.60 bid/ask price. Suppose that the next day the announced earnings news is great and the option price jumps to $0.60/$0.80. If you buy the option at the middle of the bid/ask, or at $0.50, and sell it the next day also at the mid-price of $0.70, you make a 40% gain in one day. However, if you have to take the ask price when you buy and sell at the bid price, your return is zero before transaction costs and negative after. Because of the poor liquidity that is often found in options markets, the latter scenario is not uncommon. On the other hand, the impact of the bid-ask spread for Decile 10 options is much less damaging. Assume that an average option in Decile 10 has $5.20/$5.60 bid/ask. The next day the option reacts to strong earnings news and jumps to $7.35/$7.75. The investment return calculated using the mid-price is also 40%, but even if you have to take the worst side of each trade (i.e., buying at the ask and selling at the bid), your return is still a respectable 31%.

Puts

Table 3.3 lists the distribution of Absolute Bid-Ask Spread and Percentage Bid-Ask Spread for the puts. The mean (median) Absolute Bid-Ask Spread is $0.25 ($0.25), and the mean (median) Percentage Bid-Ask Spread is 18.74% (14.81%). Overall, the distributions of the two bid-ask spread measures for the puts are very similar to those for the calls. The impact of the bid-ask spread on investment performance is significant for the puts as well. On average, the option price, measured by the midpoint of the bid/ask, has to go up 18.74% for a bid-ask taker to break even. The negative impact is at least 5.88% for more than 90% of options.

Table 3.3 Absolute and Percentage Bid-Ask Spread of Puts

	Absolute Bid-Ask Spread	Percentage Bid-Ask Spread
Mean	$0.25	18.74%
Minimum	$0.01	0.35%
10th Percentile	$0.10	5.88%
25th Percentile	$0.15	9.23%
Median	$0.25	14.81%
75th Percentile	$0.25	24.00%
90th Percentile	$0.40	36.36%
Maximum	$5.00	171.13%

We also analyze the interaction of the Absolute Bid-Ask Spread and the bid price in determining the Percentage Bid-Ask Spread for the put options. Table 3.4 presents the mean and median Absolute and Percentage Bid-Ask Spreads for the ten decile portfolios sorted by the bid price of the puts. The results are similar to those of the calls.

Table 3.4 Absolute and Percentage Bid-Ask Spread, by Put Bid-Price Deciles

Decile	Bid-Price		Absolute Bid-Ask Spread		Percentage Bid-Ask Spread	
	Mean	Median	Mean	Median	Mean	Median
1	0.41	0.40	0.22	0.20	0.40	0.40
2	0.61	0.60	0.22	0.20	0.29	0.31
3	0.77	0.75	0.21	0.20	0.23	0.22
4	0.96	0.95	0.22	0.20	0.20	0.19
5	1.17	1.15	0.22	0.20	0.17	0.17
6	1.40	1.40	0.22	0.20	0.14	0.14
7	1.69	1.69	0.23	0.20	0.12	0.11
8	2.05	2.05	0.27	0.25	0.12	0.11
9	2.62	2.60	0.31	0.30	0.11	0.10
10	5.00	4.00	0.42	0.38	0.08	0.08

The mean (median) bid price of the puts increases from $0.41 ($0.40) for Decile 1 to $5.00 ($4.00) for Decile 10, representing a more than ten-fold increase. However, the mean (median) Absolute Bid-Ask Spread only increases from $0.22 ($0.20) for Decile 1 to $0.42 ($0.38) for Decile 10. Again, the Absolute Bid-Ask Spread is sticky, maintaining about the same level from Decile 1 to Decile 7. As a result, the Percentage Bid-Ask Spread is much higher for Decile 1 than for Decile 10. The mean (median) Percentage Bid-Ask Spread is 40% (40%) for Decile 1 and 8% (8%) for Decile 10. Figure 3.2 depicts the inverse relationship between the Absolute Bid-Ask Spread and the Percentage Bid-Ask Spread.

These numbers again point out that the bid-ask spread is a major concern, particularly when the bid price is low. On average, the drag on investment performance from the bid-ask spread is an astounding 40% for the low bid-price options in Decile 1, creating a serious head wind for any strategy to generate a respectable return after factoring in the bid-ask spread.

It is worth noting that we do not advocate avoiding all options with low bid prices. *In general*, options with low bid prices tend to have larger Percentage Bid-Ask Spreads primarily due to the stickiness of the Absolute Bid-Ask Spreads. However, the key variable to consider is the Percentage Bid-Ask Spread. As long as this variable is small and the transaction cost is low, there is little importance in distinguishing low-bid-price options from high-bid-price options.

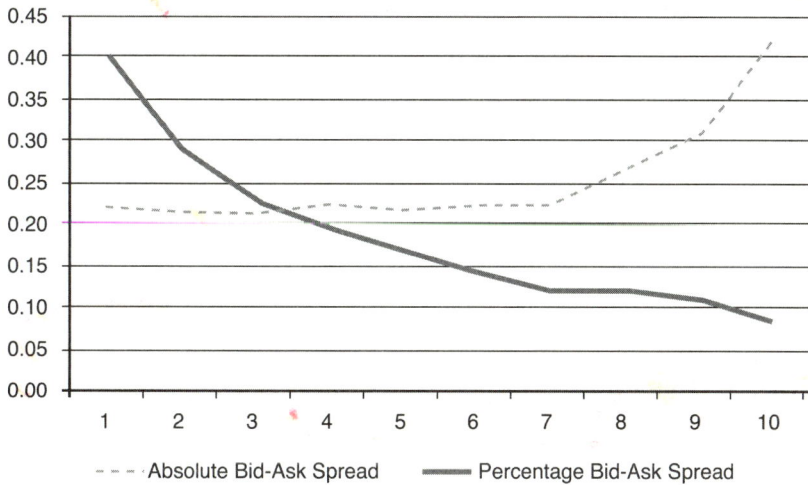

Figure 3.2 Mean Absolute and Percentage Bid-Ask Spread, by Put Bid-Price deciles.

The Impact of Different Bid-Ask Spread Assumptions on Performance

The next topic of interest is the impact of different bid-ask spread assumptions on the profitability of simulated trading. We compare three bid-ask spread possibilities with differing degrees of aggressiveness:

- *Mid-price:* Options are executed at the midpoint of the bid/ask spread.
- *75% Rule:* Options are bought at the average of the ask and the mid-price (i.e., you take 75% of the bid-ask spread) and sold at the average of the bid and the mid-price (i.e., you take 75% of the bid-ask spread).

- *Worst-price:* Options are bought at the ask and sold at the bid (i.e., you take 100% of the bid-ask spread in the round-trip transactions).

Of the three potential trade executions, the *mid-price* execution is most aggressive because it assumes you are able to execute your trade at a price significantly better than the market demands—when the market asks for a certain purchase price, you are able to purchase at a much better price; similarly, when the market bids for a certain sales price, you are able to sell at a much better price. On the other hand, the *worst-price* execution is the most conservative because it assumes you execute your trades at the worst possible price—whatever the market bids or asks for, you comply at that price, paying the highest amount for purchases and selling at the lowest prices. Between these two extremes, a more realistic assumption for trading is what we call the 75% *rule* (because the executed price is assumed to lie in the middle of the midpoint and the worst price). We believe the 75% rule is a reasonable compromise between the mid-price and worst-price scenarios. This 75% rule assumes that you do not simply take the worst price of what the market offers (that is, you do not place market orders). However, it also does not commit the crime of assuming that you will always be able to execute at the midpoint of the bid-ask spread, because this is far from guaranteed and seldom occurs outside of the most liquid markets. Instead, the 75% rule assumes that you are diligent and patient enough to enter only trades in which a decent price can be procured—if you enter a limit order adhering to the 75% rule, some of your trades will simply not execute, which you might generally view as a better alternative than entering the position at the worst possible prices.

We start with an example to show how these different bid-ask-spread assumptions can greatly change the profitability of a trade.

We assume that the trade is entered at the end of the day before the announcement and held for two days because, with our end-of-day pricing data, it is unclear whether a company announces earnings before markets open or after markets close.

In the after hours of April 11, 2003, Popular, Inc. (NASDAQ: BPOP), the largest bank in Puerto Rico, announced its first-quarter earnings for fiscal year 2003. The stock went down –0.52% on April 11, 2003; but the earnings news was positive so the next day it went up 1.46%. BPOP closed at $34.40 on April 10, 2003, and so you bought a 05/17/2003 $35 call option (read: call option with $35 strike price and May 17, 2003, expiration date). At the close on April 10, 2003, the bid/ask for the call was $0.60/$0.85. Two days later when the position was closed, the option's bid/ask was $0.70/$0.95. The returns of the trade under the three bid-ask spread assumptions (before transaction costs) are as follows:

- *Mid-price:* 13.79% (this assumes the trade is entered at the midpoint of the bid, $0.60, and the ask, $0.85, [= $0.725] and exited at the midpoint of the bid, $0.70, and the ask, $0.95, [=$0.825]).
- *75% Rule:* –3.18% (this assumes the trade is entered at the midpoint of the mid-price, $0.725, and the ask, $0.85, [= $0.7875] and exited at the midpoint of the bid, $0.70, and the mid-price, $0.825, [= $0.7625]).
- *Worst-price:* –17.65% (this assumes the trade is entered at the ask, $0.85, and exited at the bid, $0.70).

The mid-price assumption suggests that the trade was a great success, whereas the worst-price assumption suggests that it was a disaster. The 75% rule shows a modest loss, which was a more likely result in real trading.

How Do Bid-Ask Spread Assumptions Impact the Returns of Calls?

Different bid-ask spread assumptions have a large impact on the returns of a large sample of calls. Our sample included the 25,060 profitable trades of the original 58,666 calls, assuming mid-price execution. (We examine only profitable trades to demonstrate how many supposed winning trades turn to losses when more conservative bid-ask-spread assumptions are made.) If we assume the 75% rule, 9% of these trades become unprofitable. The portion of unprofitable trades increases to 17% if we assume the worst price rule. The difference in returns between different bid-ask spread assumptions is quite large.

To examine how the impact varies with the Percentage Bid-Ask Spread, we sort the trades into ten equal-size decile portfolios based on the Percentage Bid-Ask Spread. Figure 3.3 shows the mean returns of the calls for the deciles with the three different execution assumptions. Detailed data are provided in Table A3.1 in the "Appendix" section at the end of the chapter.

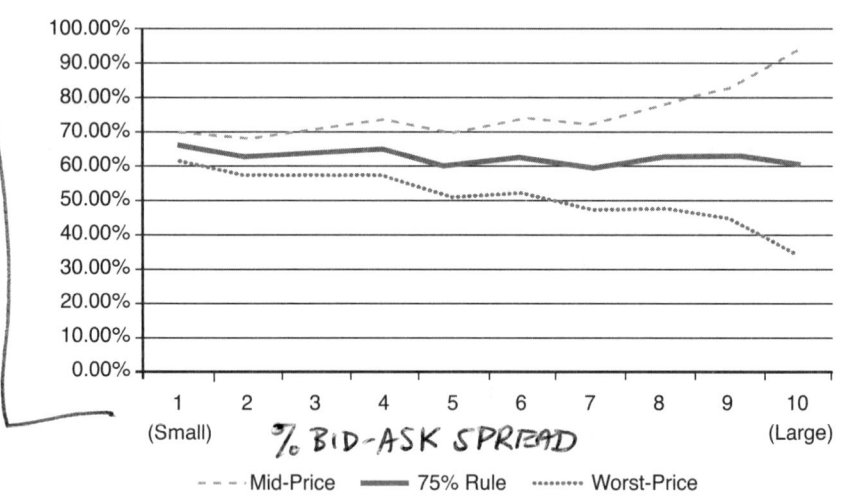

Figure 3.3 Mean returns of calls with different execution assumptions.

Several interesting observations emerge from the data. First, if we assume (aggressive) mid-price execution, the mean returns of the decile portfolios are around 70% for the first seven deciles and then increase monotonically to 93% for the top decile, even though the Percentage Bid-Ask Spread increased dramatically from 3.93% for Decile 1 to 49.29% for Decile 10. Therefore, if you can execute at mid-prices, you do not have to care about the bid-ask spread at all. If anything, you prefer larger bid-ask spreads. Second, when the moderate 75% rule is assumed, mean returns are about flat for all deciles. However, the return difference between the 75% rule and the mid-price assumption increases from about 4% for Decile 1 to roughly 33% for Decile 10. Finally, when the (conservative) worst-price execution is assumed, the mean returns monotonically decrease with the percentage bid-ask spread. For Decile 10, returns with mid-price execution are three times as large as that with worst-price execution. This evidence highlights the extreme sensitivity of returns to different bid-ask spread assumptions.

How Do Bid-Ask Spread Assumptions Impact the Returns of Puts?

The story for puts is very similar to that for calls. We examined 22,507 profitable long puts when the mid-price was assumed. Eleven percent of these trades became unprofitable when using the 75% rule, and 21% were unprofitable with worst price orders.

Figure 3.4 shows the mean returns for the ten equal-size decile portfolios based on the Percentage Bid-Ask Spread under the three different bid-ask assumptions. Detailed data are provided in Table A3.2 in the "Appendix" section. The results were very similar to those for the calls. When the mid-price was assumed, bid-ask spreads were directly correlated with the profitability of these puts (of course, correlation does not necessarily mean causation). When the 75% rule was assumed, the mean returns of the puts slightly declined as the bid-ask spread widened. The impact of the bid-ask spread was significantly negative when the worst-price was assumed. For the 10% of options with the highest percentage bid-ask spread, the mean return with the mid-price assumption was more than four times that of the worst-price assumption.

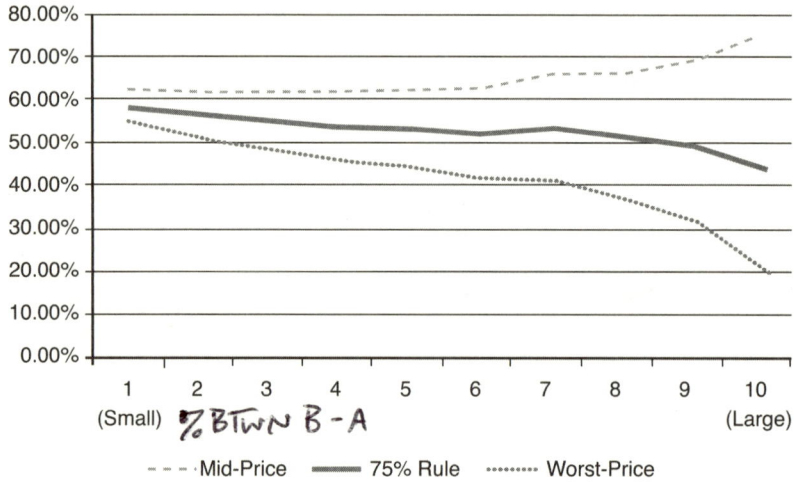

Figure 3.4 Mean returns of puts with different execution assumptions.

The Takeaway

Bid-ask spreads in the option market are a nontrivial cost, and different assumptions on execution prices can have a material impact on a strategy's performance. In later chapters, we limit our investible universe to options with low bid-ask spreads and assume the moderate 75% rule for execution. Such measures are necessary—and we strongly advise against considering the aggressive midpoint assumption—to ensure that simulation results will be relatively close to what you can achieve in the real world.

Endnotes

1. For each contract, the 3-cent-per-share round-trip transaction cost translates to $3 per contract. So if you trade the required minimum ten contracts, the round-trip commission is $30, about the average among major brokerages.
2. We assume the Absolute Bid-Ask Spread remains the same after the option price jumps, which closely matches reality.

Appendix

Table A3.1 Mean Returns of Calls with Different Execution Assumptions

Percentage Bid-Ask Spread Decile	Percentage Bid-Ask Spread	Mid-Price	75% Rule	Worst-Price
1 (Small)	3.93%	68.93%	65.05%	61.24%
2	6.71%	68.01%	62.57%	57.30%
3	8.92%	70.14%	63.27%	56.69%
4	11.02%	72.96%	64.63%	56.74%
5	13.05%	69.80%	60.26%	51.31%
6	15.35%	73.30%	62.26%	52.01%
7	18.17%	72.03%	59.34%	47.71%
8	22.59%	77.76%	61.90%	47.65%
9	29.82%	83.00%	62.42%	44.53%
10 (Large)	49.29%	93.42%	60.57%	34.53%

Table A3.2 Mean Returns of Puts with Different Execution Assumptions

Percentage Bid-Ask Spread Decile	Percentage Bid-Ask Spread	Mid-Price	75% Rule	Worst-Price
1 (Small)	4.15%	61.87%	58.11%	54.43%
2	6.89%	61.90%	56.60%	51.49%
3	9.12%	61.37%	54.63%	48.18%
4	11.34%	61.82%	53.66%	45.94%
5	13.44%	62.37%	52.94%	44.10%
6	15.79%	62.89%	51.96%	41.83%
7	18.84%	65.91%	53.06%	41.32%
8	23.46%	66.44%	50.75%	36.72%
9	30.48%	68.72%	49.02%	31.95%
10 (Large)	50.23%	75.16%	44.22%	19.79%

Part II
Options Strategies for Earnings Announcements: Let the Data Speak

In the previous chapters, you discovered the exciting trading opportunities for earnings announcements, potential option strategies you can put into action, and the significant liquidity risk in options trading. In this section, you will find a thorough analysis of many options strategies designed to explore various aspects of earnings announcements. The most distinct feature of this book is that we do not use anecdotal, cherry-picked examples to support or refute a view. Instead, we analyze all equity options in the U.S. from 1996 to 2009 and let the data tell the story. Some of the results may be consistent with your expectations, but many may not be. Investors should not adopt any strategy, no matter how persuasive it sounds, without seeing strong, supportive evidence first. The past might not represent the future, but being ignorant of the historical evidence is dangerous.

In Chapters 4 and 5 you will find the results of directional trades. Chapter 4 discusses bullish trades, and Chapter 5 investigates bearish trades. Chapters 6 and 7 cover volatility trades. Chapter 6 deals with long volatility trades, and Chapter 7 examines short volatility trades. Chapter 8 analyzes the strategy of buying volatility before earnings announcements. Chapter 9 explores the post-earnings-announcement drift phenomenon using options.

4

Bullish Directional Trades

In this chapter, we empirically examine the performance of directional bullish trades around earnings announcements. The most straightforward bullish option trades are (1) long positions in calls, and (2) short positions in puts. The different risk/return profiles of these two bullish trades are notable. Namely, long call positions have unlimited upside profit potential with a limited downside risk equal to the purchase price of the option. On the other hand, short put positions have an upside equal to the price of the put shorted, but the downside has greater risks. These risks are not unlimited because a price cannot fall below zero. As we will show shortly, in the worst case, put writers have to pay seven or eight times what they receive to cover their short position.

We start with the largest 3,000 stocks in the U.S., representing 99% of the market capitalization of all publicly traded companies. We examine only stocks with earnings announcement dates and returns data, and each stock must have options listed on the exchange. Each option must have complete data to study (i.e., a strike price, an expiration date, implied volatility, and bid and ask prices). Based on the detailed analysis explained in Chapter 3, "Liquidity Risk: Bid-Ask Spreads," we include in our sample only those options meeting our liquidity requirements: (1) the percentage bid-ask spread is no greater than 10%; and (2) the bid price of the option is no smaller than $0.30. The two requirements ensure that bid-ask spreads and transaction costs do not take a large toll on the strategies' profits.

Long Calls: The Baseline Case

Table 4.1 shows the empirical distribution of all long calls. This baseline examination was for the nearest expiration month, at-the-money or near-the-money call options, which means the strike price is less than 5% away from the underlying equity price. The baseline case enters each position at the closing price one day prior to the earnings announcement and exits the position at the closing price one day after the earnings announcement. This is a trade lasting two trading days. The baseline test consists of 10,901 observations.

Table 4.1 Performance of Long Calls: The Baseline Case

Execution Assumption	Mean	Minimum	1st Quartile	Median	3rd Quartile	Maximum
Mid-Price	2.31%	−99.43%	−53.25%	−13.89%	37.93%	1004.92%
75% Rule	−1.03%	−99.72%	−55.56%	−16.95%	34.13%	970.40%
Worst-Price	−4.25%	−100.00%	−57.69%	−20.00%	30.00%	937.50%

As discussed in Chapter 3, a significant choice made in this analysis is the selection of an entry/exit point regarding the bid-ask spread. Three bid-ask spread assumptions are considered: (1) the *mid-price*, which is the midpoint of the bid-ask spread, (2) the *worst-price*, where entry and exit occur at the offer price (i.e., buy at the ask and sell at the bid), and (3) the *75% rule*, which is the average of the midpoint price and the worst-case price. To test the sensitivity of the long call strategy's performance to different bid-ask spread assumptions, we present results for all three scenarios. (We do not consider the alternative of choosing the best price, where you enter the long call trade at the bid and exit the trade at the going asking price. This optimistic bent in analysis would wreak havoc on actual trades because it is very unrealistic.)

Table 4.1 shows that the average two-day return from a long call position surrounding earnings announcements was 2.31% if all trades were executed at the midpoint of the bid-ask spread. However, a closer look into the distribution of these returns reveals that the median is −13.89%, suggesting that well over half of the long call trades are losing strategies. The 3rd Quartile and maximum returns reveal that the 2.31% average returns were driven by the right tail of the distribution—the 3rd Quartile return was 37.93%, which means that a full 25% of the trades had returns higher than 37.93%.

The previous analysis considered trade entry/exit at the midpoint of the bid-ask spread. As much as traders would like mid-price execution, this is unrealistic. The next lines of inquiry consider more realistic execution assumptions: the worst-price and the 75% rule. When more realistic execution prices are assumed, even average returns from long call trades are negative. Specifically, when trading is done at the 75% mark of the bid-ask spread (i.e., the average of the mid-price and the worst-price), the average returns are −1.03%; and the median return is −16.95%, which by construction is worse than the midpoint analysis. Indeed, assuming the 75% rule, only 40.0% of long call positions were profitable. Lastly, the average return from taking the worst-price is −4.25%, much lower than the 2.31% from mid-price assumptions. Similar conclusions apply to the median and the percentile distribution of returns.

Short Puts: The Baseline Case

In Table 4.2, an alternative bullish strategy is studied: the short put. We first consider the midpoint analysis. The average short put trade had a return of 1.68%. The median return was 15.96%. The fact that the median return was much larger than the mean return suggests that the left tail of the distribution of returns (i.e., the losers) dragged down the averages. This makes sense because the short put strategy has a capped upside return, and a large downside exposure (which is the opposite of the long call strategy of Table 4.1). You can verify this by the fact that the maximum return from this two-day short put strategy was 98.96%, whereas the worst-case scenario had a negative return of –679.17%.

Table 4.2 Performance of Short Puts: The Baseline Case

Execution Assumption	Mean	Minimum	1st Quartile	Median	3rd Quartile	Maximum
Mid-Price	1.68%	–679.17%	–30.00%	15.96%	52.08%	98.96%
75% Rule	–1.77%	–702.13%	–34.21%	12.95%	49.71%	98.62%
Worst-Price	–5.33%	–726.09%	–38.71%	9.68%	47.44%	98.41%

An examination into the trades executed under the 75% rule and the worst-price assumptions reveals similar results. Assuming the 75% rule, the average return of the short put strategy dropped to –1.77%, which is not surprising since the 75% rule assumes worse prices on both the entry and the exit trades compared to the mid-price analysis. The median returns were positive under the 75% rule, 12.95%. In fact, the median returns are still positive even with the worst-price scenario, 9.68%. Assuming the 75% rule, 57.7% of the short put trades are profitable, compared to just 40% for the long calls. Hence, the short put strategy is superior to the long call strategy from a hit ratio (likelihood of profitable trades) perspective.

Time Series Analysis

Figure 4.1 shows the long call strategy using the 75% rule pricing—now the standard assumption—on a yearly basis. Detailed data are provided in Table A4.1 in the "Appendix" section later in this chapter. Figure 4.1 shows that the *average* returns of the long calls were positive in five years: 1999, 2001, 2003, 2004, and 2005. However, the other nine years had on average negative returns. The median returns were always negative, regardless of the year examined. This suggests that less than 50% of long calls are profitable in any given year.

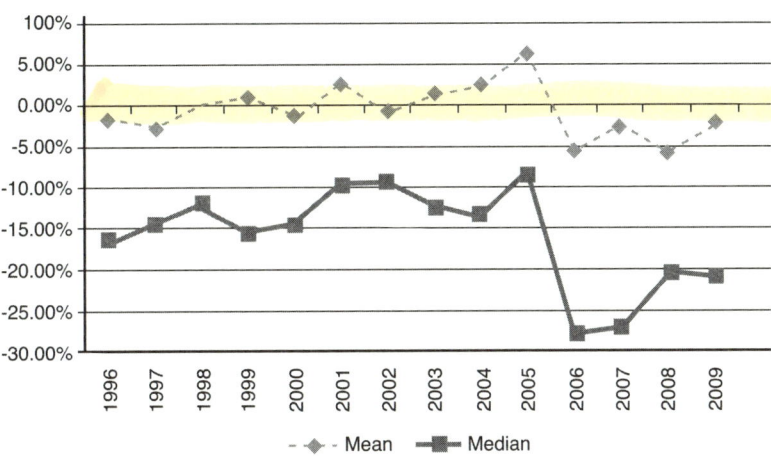

Figure 4.1 Annual performance of the long call strategy.

Figure 4.2 shows yearly results for the short put strategy using the 75% rule prices. More detailed data about the figure are provided in Table A4.2 in the "Appendix" section. The mean returns were profitable in five years (2001, 2003, 2005, 2008, and 2009). However, more than half of the short put trades were profitable in all years, as evidenced by the consistently positive median returns. Moreover, there seems to be an upward trend in returns of the short put strategy over the years.

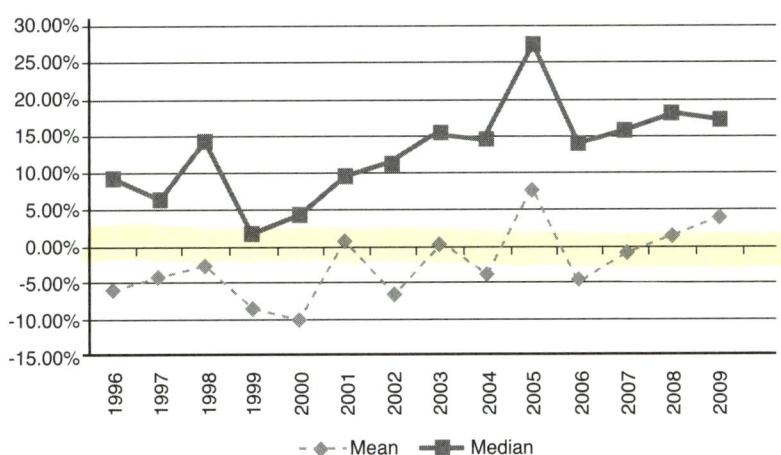

Figure 4.2 Annual performance of the short put strategy.

These annual results further validate the findings from the entire sample: Long calls are on average losers, whereas the probability of success is much higher for short puts.

Turning the Dials

So far, the results reported were for the baseline tests: near-the-money strike prices, nearest expiration dates, and two-day holding periods. We examine the impact of adjusting each of these parameters on the results, which allows for you to gauge how sensitive each assumption is on the profitability of a given strategy. The study starts with tweaking the strike price, followed by tweaking the expiration date, and then the holding period.

Out-of-the-Money Options

So far, selected trades used at-the-money or near-the-money strike prices. If the underlying equity were trading at $10.20, we would select a strike price of $10. Our default screening allowed for a 5% deviation in price relative to strike price. What if we choose a strike price further out, such as $11? Our "out-of-the-money" tests require the underlying equity price to be 5% to 10% away from the option's strike price. (We cap our out-of-the-money tests to 10% because strike prices more than 10% out-of-the-money tend to be thinly traded, making the spreads wider, which in turn makes historical examination of trade profitability less reliable.) In Table 4.3, the long call strategy is reexamined, assuming selection of out-of-the-money strikes. All other aspects of the trades were not changed; options still have the nearest expiration date and a two-day holding period. Instead of presenting results with all three execution assumptions, we report only the 75% rule results. We also included results from the baseline trades (near-the-money) for comparison purpose.[1]

Table 4.3 Performance of Long Calls: Out-of-the-Money Strike

Strike Price	Mean	Minimum	1st Quartile	Median	3rd Quartile	Maximum
NTM	–1.45%	–99.72%	–54.12%	–15.96%	31.94%	528.12%
OTM	–2.76%	–99.46%	–72.73%	–37.10%	25.64%	2316.67%

The results suggest that choosing strikes that are further out-of-the-money leads to a more extreme return distribution. On average, the OTM strategy produced a –2.76% return compared to the NTM strategy of –1.45%. The median return was also much worse for the OTM strategy than for the NTM strategy (–37.10% versus –15.96%). In fact, buying OTM calls was profitable only 32.9% of the time, which was worse than the 40.0% hit ratio for NTM calls. When the trading strategy was profitable, the OTM strategy produced more positive returns relative to the NTM strategy, and vice versa for negative returns. The OTM strategy behaved as a leveraged version of the NTM strategy: It amplified all news, good or bad.

Table 4.4 reports a similar comparison for short puts. The results were similar: The OTM strategy acts as a leveraged version of the NTM strategy. Shorting OTM puts was profitable 64.0% of the time, compared with 57.7% of the time for NTM puts. These results were not surprising because OTM strikes are more difficult to reach. But the empirical finding that 64.0% of short puts were profitable stresses how much you have on your side for such plays.

Table 4.4 Performance of Short Puts: Out-of-the-Money Strike

Strike Price	Mean	Minimum	1st Quartile	Median	3rd Quartile	Maximum
NTM	–0.58%	–664.82%	–32.88%	13.51%	48.42%	98.62%
OTM	–0.53%	–2350.00%	–26.09%	25.00%	59.00%	98.64%

It is worth noting that OTM strike prices have a different impact on the extreme returns of the two bullish trades (i.e., long calls and short puts) due to the different risk/return profiles of the two trades. Specifically, OTM strike prices significantly boost the extreme positive returns for the long calls, although they have no impact on the extreme negative returns (because when earnings announcement returns are sufficiently negative, the calls lose essentially all their value no matter what the strike price is). The opposite is true for the short puts. In our sample, the maximum return for the long calls is more than three times higher with the OTM strikes than with the NTM strikes (2316.67% versus 528.12%). For the short put strategy, the minimum return is almost three times worse with the OTM strikes than with the NTM strikes (−2350.00% versus −664.82%).

Further Expiration Dates

In the next set of tables, another aspect of these trades was tested. All the baseline tests used the nearest expiration months. For example, if the earnings announcement date was February 27, we would choose the nearest-month expiration option, which (if available) would be a March expiration. In the next set of tables, we reexamined all of our results assuming that we chose an expiration at least two months away. All other aspects of the trades did not change. Only the 75% rule results were included.

In Table 4.5, the top line is the baseline case of using the nearest-month expiration contract for long calls. The bottom line is for an expiration month at least two months away. All the returns were muted for the further-month options—positive returns were less positive, and negative returns were less negative. 42.8% of all trades with further expiration dates were profitable, compared with 40.0% for the baseline case. In short, extending expiration dates translates to a lower response coefficient. Given a price change of the underlying equity, price swings of the options are less pronounced because the drop in implied volatility is less dramatic. Though typically the time decay of an option is much more pronounced in the nearer months relative to the further months, time decay is unlikely to have a significant impact on our results because the holding period was only two trading days. Thus, though time decay contributed to the differences, the main reason for the observed results was the smaller decrease in implied volatility of options with further expiration dates.

Table 4.5 Performance of Long Calls: Further Expiration Dates

Expiration Date	Mean	Minimum	1st Quartile	Median	3rd Quartile	Maximum
Near Month	−1.49%	−99.72%	−56.56%	−17.68%	33.85%	970.40%
Further Month	−0.80%	−98.66%	−36.05%	8.28%	25.16%	352.05%

Table 4.6 shows similar evidence for the short put strategy. The returns were muted for options with further expiration dates—positive returns were less positive, and negative returns were less negative. Only 53.3% of short puts were profitable when the expiration date was extended, compared to the 57.7% profitable trades for the baseline short put case.

Table 4.6 Performance of Short Puts: Further Expiration Dates

Expiration Date	Mean	Minimum	1st Quartile	Median	3rd Quartile	Maximum
Near Month	−2.04%	−702.13%	−34.97%	12.94%	49.66%	98.62%
Further Month	−2.75%	−415.56%	−25.41%	3.82%	29.10%	97.89%

Increasing the Holding Period

In the next set of tables, the holding period of baseline trades was extended. For the baseline trades of Tables 4.1 and 4.2, each position was entered at the closing price one day prior to the earnings announcement and exited at the closing price one day after the earnings announcement, for a two-day holding period. We now extend the holding period by three days, creating a five-day holding period. There are two forces at work when the holding period is extended. First, if the market underreacts to news in earnings announcements,[2] more profits would be captured by holding onto the winning trades longer. Second, time decay works against long positions and works for short positions. For long calls, the two forces compete with each other, whereas for the short put options, they work together.

Table 4.7 presents the results for the long calls. The average return of the five-day holding period was much worse than the baseline two-day holding period: –3.81% versus –0.43%. The median return was much worse too (–27.40% for the five-day window versus –15.74% for the two-day window). 38.1% of the long call trades were profitable with the five-day holding period, less than the 40.0% for the two-day holding period. Examining the 3rd Quartile returns, the five-day holding period had more positive returns, indicating that there might be some stock price drift after earnings announcements. However, the results suggest that on average time decay overwhelms the drift for long call trades, so traders with long call positions are better off with a shorter holding period.

Table 4.7 Performance of Long Call Options: Longer Holding Period

Holding Period	Mean	Minimum	1st Quartile	Median	3rd Quartile	Maximum
Two Days	–0.43%	–99.72%	–52.23%	–15.74%	33.85%	970.40%
Five Days	–3.81%	–99.76%	–68.85%	–27.40%	36.74%	879.27%

We present the results of extending the holding period for the short put strategy in Table 4.8. Both the mean and median returns were higher when holding onto the short put for five days instead of the baseline two days. The mean return of the short put strategy with a five-day holding period jumped to 3.56% from 0.10%. The percentage of profitable trades increased to 62% from 57.7% when the holding period was extended from two days to five days. The evidence is consistent with what we predicted: Both drift and time decay worked in favor of extending the holding period for short puts.

Table 4.8 Performance of Short Put Options: Longer Holding Period

Holding Period	Mean	Minimum	1st Quartile	Median	3rd Quartile	Maximum
Two Days	0.10%	–624.73%	–31.48%	12.95%	48.32%	98.54%
Five Days	3.56%	–813.85%	–34.93%	25.62%	64.04%	98.98%

Thought Experiment: Knowing Earnings Announcement Returns

The final set of analyses examines how these strategies would perform if we knew what the earnings announcement returns were going to be ahead of time. This provides a sense of the *potential* profitability of the trades. For example, if the earnings announcement return is 5%, what is the potential profit from a long call or short put? Understanding the potential profitability of your trades helps you better understand the possible upside/downside and allows for a better cost-benefit analysis of each trade you take on.

To perform this analysis, we sorted all the observations based on two-day earnings announcement returns into ten equal-sized decile portfolios. We then examined the distribution of option strategies' returns for each decile portfolio. For instance, in Decile 1, we had the observations with the worst (most negative) two-day earnings announcement equity returns, and in Decile 10, we had the observations with the best (most positive) earnings announcement equity returns. How did long calls and short puts do in each of these decile portfolios?

Figure 4.3 shows the mean and median long call returns based on these ranked portfolios. Detailed data are provided in Table A4.3 in the "Appendix" section. The labels of the x-axis show the range of the equity earnings announcement returns for each decile portfolio.

For example, for Decile 1, all returns were less than −9%. For Decile 10, all returns were greater than 10%. By construction, the returns to the long call trades increased with the earnings announcement returns. For example, the mean (median) return of the long call strategy was −79.99% (−83.62%) for Decile 1, and 140.28% (118.42%) for Decile 10.

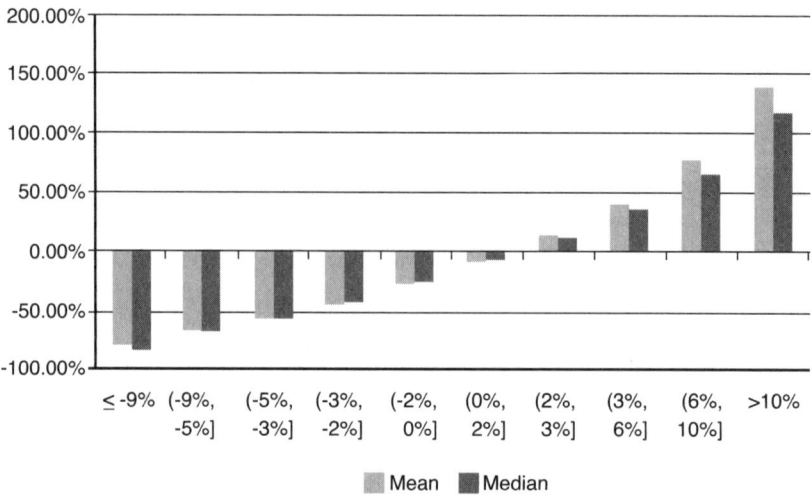

Figure 4.3 Performance of long calls by earnings announcement returns.

Perusing the ranked portfolios, you can see that long call strategies are unprofitable for the first six deciles, representing 60% of the sample. The most interesting and perhaps counterintuitive result is for Decile 6, in which the earnings announcement returns are positive but smaller than 2%. However, both the mean and median returns for the long call strategy are quite *negative* for this group (−8.05% and −6.90%, respectively). The evidence highlights the large tolls taken by volatility collapse and, to a lesser degree, time decay on the long call trades.

The graph also provides a general sense of how much gain or loss you should expect given the realized earnings announcement returns. For example, if the earnings announcement return is somewhere between −5% and −3%, the average loss for the long call trades is −57%, quite a large loss for two days. On the other hand, if the earnings announcement return is somewhere between 3% and 6%, the average gain is 42% in two days.

If we consider only the trades in which the underlying equity earnings announcement returns were positive, buying calls is profitable 78.9% of the time. Though this is a high percentage, it's more informative to state the opposite: Even when the earnings announcement return is positive, buying calls can lose money 21.1% of the time! And obviously, when the earnings announcement return is negative, almost all long call trades lose money.

A similar analysis for the short put strategy is presented in Figure 4.4. Detailed data for Figure 4.4 are provided in Table A4.4 in the "Appendix" section. The mean returns of the short put strategy increased with the earnings announcement returns as well. Compared to the results for the long call strategy in which six decile portfolios were unprofitable, six decile portfolios were profitable for the short put strategy. Another counterintuitive result is that the short put strategy actually turns in profits when the earnings announcement returns are slightly negative. The portfolio with negative earnings announcements returns between −2% and 0% (Decile 5), the mean returns for the short put strategy were 3.69% and 2.43%, respectively. The long call strategy, on the other hand, was slaughtered in this portfolio with an average return of −27.68% and a median return of −17.12%. Similar differences between the two strategies were observed when the earnings announcement returns were between 0% and 2% (Decile 6). When the short put strategy was applied to stocks in this portfolio, the mean and median returns were 23.64% and 21.29%, respectively, and even the 1st Quartile return was a large 13.48%. However, the average return for the long call strategy applied to the same stocks was −8.05% and the median return was −6.90%. The large differences in returns between the two strategies was striking because all other aspects of the two strategies, such as the underlying stock returns, strike price, and holding period, were identical. Two factors explain the differences in performance between the two strategies: Volatility collapse and time decay. Both factors favored the short put strategy and worked against the long call strategy.

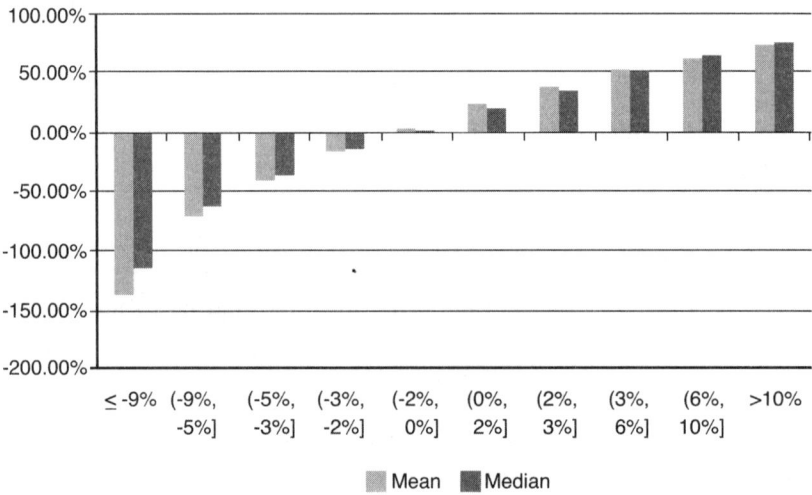

Figure 4.4 Performance of short puts by earnings announcement returns.

The short put strategy was more profitable than the long call strategy unless the earnings announcement returns were at extremes (Decile 1 and Decile 10). To gauge the potential gains/losses from the strategies, we examined the mean and median returns for Decile 3 and Decile 7. When the earnings announcement return was somewhere between –5% and –3% (Decile 3), the average loss for short put trades was –41.43%, whereas the average gain was 52.14% if the earnings announcement return was somewhere between 3% and 6% (Decile 7). Both numbers are much better than their counterparts of the long call strategy (–56.71% and 46.73%, respectively). When the underlying equity returns were positive, selling puts was profitable 99.2% of the time, versus the 78.9% hit ratio for the long call trades.

The Takeaway

When assuming mid-price execution, the average returns of both the long call and short put strategies are positive. When more conservative entry/exit prices (i.e., the 75% rule and the worst-price) are assumed, the mean returns of both strategies turn negative. These results suggest that after paying the bid-ask spread, the long call and short put strategies have small losses on average.

However, the distribution of possible returns paints a different picture for the long call and short put strategies. The median return of the long call strategy is persistently negative, but the median return of the short put strategy is persistently positive, as evidenced by the time-series analysis. 57.7% of the short puts are profitable, compared to 40% for the long calls.

Changing the parameters of the option trades has a large impact on the results. Judging by median returns that are not affected by extreme scenarios, using out-of-the-money instead of near-the-money strike prices exacerbates the losses from long calls, but improves the profitability of short puts. Extending the expiration dates makes the returns to both long calls and short puts more muted because options with further-month expiration dates have smaller decreases in implied volatility. Increasing the holding period has a large negative impact on long calls, but greatly boosts the performance of short puts because time decay works in favor of the short puts but against the long calls.

Further analysis shows that, contrary to conventional wisdom, the long calls are actually losing money on average when the earnings announcement returns are slightly positive (smaller than 2%). Also in contrast to common sense, the short puts are on average profitable when the earnings announcement returns are slightly negative (larger than –2%).

Because of the different risk/return profiles, option traders generally prefer to express their bullish views through long calls instead of short puts. However, all the empirical, data-driven evidence in this chapter strongly suggests that shorting puts is the more advantageous way to express bullish views. Volatility collapse after earnings announcements and time decay were both head winds for the long call strategy but tail winds for the short put strategy. The biggest risk to shorting puts is the left-tail risk that can cause large losses. A diversified portfolio and better security selection can significantly reduce the impact of this tail risk.

Endnotes

1. The baseline results in Table 4.3 are different from those in Table 4.1. This is because in Table 4.3 we require the options to have both a near-the-money strike and an out-of-the-money strike, so the sample in Table 4.3 is a subset of the sample in Table 4.1. This will be the case for all remaining tables in this chapter.

2. Academics have long documented the "post-earnings-announcement drift" phenomenon, but the main finding is about the drift in the months rather than days following earnings announcements.

Appendix

Table A4.1 Annual Performance of the Long Call Strategy

Year	Mean	1st Quartile	Median	3rd Quartile
1996	−1.77%	−47.27%	−16.47%	33.95%
1997	−2.78%	−45.00%	−14.44%	26.09%
1998	−0.19%	−45.41%	−12.08%	31.09%
1999	0.87%	−47.66%	−15.55%	31.75%

CHAPTER 4 • BULLISH DIRECTIONAL TRADES

Year	Mean	1st Quartile	Median	3rd Quartile
2000	–1.35%	–50.70%	–14.40%	32.93%
2001	2.61%	–41.52%	–9.64%	36.51%
2002	–0.75%	–48.33%	–9.37%	31.20%
2003	1.32%	–48.84%	–12.32%	34.10%
2004	2.37%	–58.63%	–13.33%	40.74%
2005	6.25%	–58.18%	–8.40%	40.91%
2006	–5.42%	–68.64%	–27.85%	30.99%
2007	–2.63%	–64.23%	–26.89%	38.83%
2008	–5.65%	–61.05%	–20.61%	32.31%
2009	–2.15%	–59.23%	–21.07%	34.67%

Table A4.2 Annual Performance of the Short Put Strategy

Year	Mean	1st Quartile	Median	3rd Quartile
1996	–5.71%	–32.53%	9.18%	50.53%
1997	–3.90%	–32.08%	6.86%	40.91%
1998	–2.42%	–30.79%	14.33%	40.54%
1999	–8.29%	–39.22%	1.60%	37.01%
2000	–9.87%	–40.28%	4.26%	40.70%
2001	0.85%	–26.58%	9.49%	40.68%
2002	–6.29%	–36.73%	11.51%	40.48%
2003	0.49%	–28.69%	15.74%	49.23%
2004	–3.66%	–38.83%	14.85%	54.96%
2005	7.74%	–21.95%	27.36%	62.83%
2006	–4.47%	–48.70%	13.95%	58.51%
2007	–0.75%	–35.48%	15.87%	57.50%
2008	1.59%	–30.68%	17.91%	54.95%
2009	4.13%	–28.99%	17.28%	52.88%

Table A4.3 Performance of Long Calls by Earnings Announcement Returns

Earnings Announcement Returns	Mean	1st Quartile	Median	3rd Quartile
≤ –9%	–79.99%	–91.67%	–83.62%	–70.41%
(–9%, –5%]	–66.85%	–80.80%	–67.82%	–53.73%
(–5%, –3%]	–56.71%	–67.60%	–56.86%	–44.70%
(–3%, –2%]	–44.99%	–55.67%	–43.23%	–32.88%
(–2%, 0%]	–27.68%	–35.77%	–25.34%	–17.12%
(0%, 2%]	–8.05%	–15.29%	–6.90%	0.68%
(2%, 3%]	14.69%	1.78%	12.71%	24.58%
(3%, 6%]	41.63%	20.49%	36.48%	56.69%
(6%, 10%]	77.42%	42.54%	66.35%	100.00%
> 10%	140.28%	82.09%	118.42%	174.03%

Table A4.4 Performance of Short Puts by Earnings Announcement Returns

Earnings Announcement Returns	Mean	1st Quartile	Median	3rd Quartile
≤ –9%	–139.70%	–176.42%	–117.74%	–77.54%
(–9%, –5%]	–70.97%	–91.78%	–62.92%	–39.13%
(–5%, –3%]	–41.43%	–56.83%	–37.31%	–21.51%
(–3%, –2%]	–17.59%	–29.33%	–15.42%	–4.72%
(–2%, 0%]	3.69%	–4.90%	2.43%	11.90%
(0%, 2%]	23.64%	13.48%	21.29%	31.51%
(2%, 3%]	38.39%	26.50%	36.80%	48.98%
(3%, 6%]	52.14%	39.83%	52.35%	64.75%
(6%, 10%]	61.71%	48.94%	63.50%	74.80%
> 10%	72.44%	61.69%	75.48%	85.12%

5

Bearish Directional Trades

The preceding chapter examined bullish directional trades. We now consider bearish directional trades. We study the most straightforward option trades: (1) long positions in puts, and (2) short positions in calls. The maximum upside of a long put position is the strike price minus the price paid (that is, if the share price were to drop to zero). A long put has a limited downside, equal to the price of the option purchased. On the other hand, short calls have an upside equal to the price of the option sold, but the downside is in theory unlimited.

The sample used in this chapter is constructed in the same way as the sample used in Chapter 4, "Bullish Directional Trades." We required that options meet two liquidity requirements: (1) the percentage bid-ask spread is no greater than 10%; (2) the bid price of the option is no smaller than $0.30.

Long Puts: The Baseline Case

Table 5.1 shows the empirical distribution for the returns of all long puts. The baseline examination was for near-the-money puts (strike price being less than 5% away from the underlying equity price) with the nearest expiration dates. In the baseline case we assumed that we would enter each position at the closing price one day prior to the earnings announcement and exit the position at the closing price one day after the earnings announcement. This is a trade lasting two trading days. Our baseline test had 10,901 observations.

Table 5.1 Performance of Long Put Options: The Baseline Case

Execution Assumption	Mean	Minimum	1st Quartile	Median	3rd Quartile	Maximum
Mid-Price	−1.68%	−98.96%	−52.08%	−15.96%	30.00%	679.17%
75% Rule	−5.01%	−99.48%	−54.30%	−18.87%	26.06%	657.14%
Worst-Price	−8.23%	−100.00%	−56.41%	−21.74%	22.22%	636.00%

Similar to the previous chapter, to test the sensitivity of our results, we present results for each of three bid-ask spread assumptions: (1) the *mid-price*, which is the midpoint of the bid-ask spread, (2) the *worst-price*, where we enter and exit at the price offered (i.e., buy at the ask and sell at the bid), and (3) the *75% rule*, which is the average of the midpoint price and the worst-case price.

Table 5.1 shows that the average two-day return from a long put position surrounding earnings announcements was −1.68%, assuming that all trades were executed at the midpoint of the bid-ask spread. A closer look into the distribution of these returns reveals that the median return was −15.96%, suggesting that well over half of the long put trades lost money. The return distribution was skewed with some large positive returns in the right tail. For example, the maximum return was 679% and more than 25% of the trades had returns higher than 30%. On the other side of the distribution, 25% of the trades lost more than half of their premium in two days. Overall, buying puts indiscriminately was a losing trade. The odds of profits were low with outright long puts: only 38.7% of the trades were profitable.

This analysis considered trade entry/exit at the midpoint of the bid-ask spread. The next lines of inquiry considered more realistic execution assumptions: the 75% rule and the worst-price. As expected, we found that performance was worse across the board. For example, assuming the 75% rule for entry/exit prices, the average return dropped to −5.01%, and the median was −18.87%. Next, if you entered and exited the positions at the prices offered by the market (worst-case), you would have lost 8.23% on average, and more than half of the time your return was lower than −21.74%.

Short Calls: The Baseline Case

Table 5.2 presents an alternative bearish trade: the short call. We again started with the mid-price assumption. Similar to the long put strategy, the average short call trade had a negative return (–2.31%). In fact, the average return for the short call trade was even lower than that for the long put trade. However, the median return for the short call trade was 13.89%, close to 30% higher than the median return for the long put trade (–15.96%). This finding is important because it indicates that (1) the odds of winning were much higher for the short call strategy than for the long put strategy and (2) the lower average return of the short call strategy was driven by the left tail of the returns distribution. For example, the minimum loss for the short call strategy was worse than –1000%. Thus, the key to a successful short call strategy is to avoid tail risk through better security selection.

Table 5.2 Performance of Short Calls: The Baseline Case

Execution Assumption	Mean	Minimum	1st Quartile	Median	3rd Quartile	Maximum
Mid-Price	–2.31%	–1004.90%	–37.93%	13.89%	53.25%	99.43%
75% Rule	–5.75%	–1041.20%	–42.27%	10.91%	51.06%	99.14%
Worst-Price	–9.32%	–1079.30%	–46.51%	7.69%	48.78%	98.84%

When considering more realistic and conservative execution assumptions, the message is not much different. The average return dropped to –5.75% (–9.32%) when the 75% rule (worst-price) was assumed. However, the median returns were still large and positive. The median return for the 75% rule was 10.91%. Even if you made no effort to get a better execution price, you still would have made money more than half of the time by selling calls indiscriminately (the median return was 7.69% when the worst-price is assumed).

Time Series Analysis

In Figure 5.1, the mean and median returns for the long put strategy using the 75% rule—which is now our standard analysis—are shown on a yearly basis. Detailed data are reported in Table A5.1 in the "Appendix" section at the end of this chapter. In the graph, the mean returns were positive in only two years: 1999 and 2000. The median returns were always negative, regardless of the year examined, suggesting that long puts are unprofitable more than half the time in every year. There is a general downward trend of both the mean and median returns over the years. This evidence suggests that, at least for the options examined, buying puts has become increasingly unprofitable, either because the earnings news tends to be better, or because implied volatility built into the puts tends to be higher.

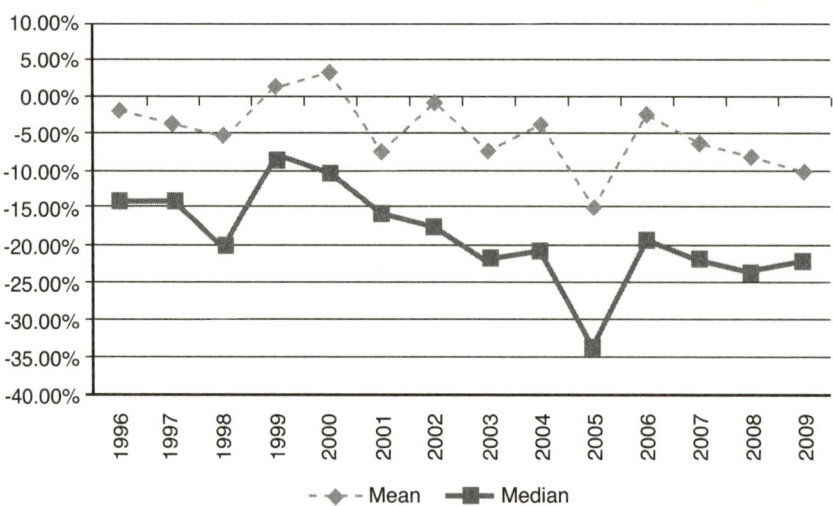

Figure 5.1 Annual performance of the long put strategy.

In Figure 5.2, we show the annual performance for the short call strategy using the 75% rule. More detailed data about the figure are provided in Table A5.2 in the "Appendix" section. In this graph, the mean returns were negative in all years, but the median returns were positive in all years. This suggests that more than half of the short call trades were profitable in all years, yet each year there were always some unexpectedly large positive earnings announcement returns. There was no downward trend in mean or median returns for the short call strategy. In fact, performance of the short call strategy seems to have increased recently, jumping higher in the last three years.

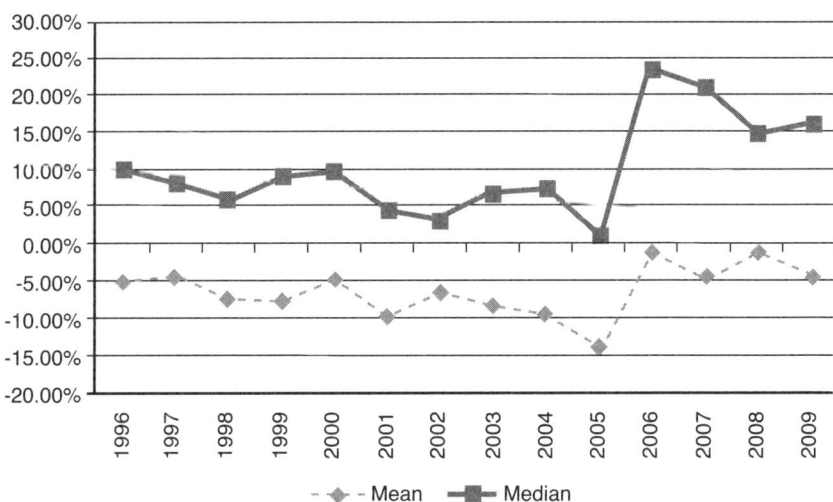

Figure 5.2 Annual performance of the short call strategy.

The annual results further validate the results for the entire sample: Long puts are on average losers, whereas the probability of success is much higher for the short call strategy.

Turning the Dials

We adjusted each of the three parameters—strike price, expiration date, and holding period—to see how the results vary. These are useful exercises because investors have to make such decisions in real trading. Our analysis starts with the strike price, followed by the expiration date and holding period.

Out-of-the-Money Options

Table 5.3 reexamines the long put strategy assuming an out-of-the-money strike price. We capped the out-of-the-moneyness to 10% of the equity price because strike prices that are more than 10% out-of-the-money tend to be thinly traded, making the spreads much wider and historical examination of trade profitability less reliable. All other aspects of the trades remained the same: we still chose options with the nearest expiration date and held them for two days. The 75% rule was assumed for execution prices. For comparison purposes, we also included results from our baseline trades (near-the-money).[1]

Table 5.3 Performance of Long Puts: Out-of-the-Money Strike

Strike Price	Mean	Minimum	1st Quartile	Median	3rd Quartile	Maximum
NTM	–5.54%	–99.14%	–52.32%	–19.30%	25.35%	636.10%
OTM	–13.10%	–99.55%	–68.22%	–36.07%	10.98%	1794.40%

The results suggest that choosing strike prices more out-of-the-money lead to a more extreme return distribution. On average, the OTM strategy produced a –13.10% return compared to the NTM strategy of –5.54%. The median returns were much worse for the OTM strategy as well (–36.07% versus –19.30%). Switching to OTM puts also made the long put strategy less likely to be profitable: The hit ratio of the long put strategy dropped from the already low 37.8% for the NTM strategy to 29.5% for the OTM strategy. At the very right tail, the OTM strategy was a leveraged version of the NTM strategy. For example, the maximum gain for the long OTM put strategy was 1794.4%, almost three times that for the long NTM put strategy. For the majority of trades, buying OTM puts was worse than buying NTM puts, as evidenced by the lower first-quartile, median, and third-quartile returns for the long OTM put strategy. The long OTM put strategies were less profitable than the long NTM puts because OTM options have lower delta and higher implied volatility than

NTM options, requiring much larger market reactions for the long positions to become profitable. (Similar evidence was documented for long call options in the previous chapter.)

Table 5.4 considers a similar comparison for short call strategies. The average OTM returns were much worse at –14.11% compared to the NTM returns of –4.57%. But the medians tell the opposite story, with returns of 23.33% for the OTM strategy versus 10.96% for the NTM strategy. OTM short call strategies were profitable 60.8% of the time, significantly better than the 55.8% hit ratio for NTM short call strategies. These results make sense because OTM calls have lower delta and higher implied volatility than NTM calls, so they can better withstand the unfavorable equity returns (in this case, the unfavorable equity return was the positive earnings announcement return) and benefit more from volatility collapse. Also, OTM calls are more likely to expire worthless than NTM calls. The worse average return for the short OTM calls was driven by a few disproportionately large losses. For example, the worst loss for shorting OTM calls was –3675%, almost seven times the worst loss for shorting NTM calls.

Table 5.4 Performance of Short Calls: Out-of-the-Money Strike

Strike Price	Mean	Minimum	1st Quartile	Median	3rd Quartile	Maximum
NTM	–4.57%	–544.30%	–39.73%	10.96%	50.06%	99.14%
OTM	–14.11%	–3675.00%	–42.53%	23.33%	62.84%	98.32%

As we discussed in previous chapters, OTM strike prices significantly boost the extreme positive returns for the long option positions, but amplify the extreme losses for the short option positions. In our sample, the maximum return for the long puts is almost two times higher with the OTM than with the NTM (1794.40% versus 636.10%). For the short put strategy, the minimum return is almost six times worse with the OTM than with the NTM (–3675.00% versus –554.30%). As a result, the average return of the short calls is much worse with the OTM than with the NTM, even though the median return comparison suggests exactly the opposite.

Further Expiration Dates

In the next set of tables, we reexamine the bearish directional trades assuming expiration dates at least two months away, in contrast to the nearest expiration month used for the baseline tests. All other aspects of the trades remained the same and we continue to assume the 75% rule for execution prices.

In Table 5.5, the top line is the baseline case of using the nearest-month expiration contract for long puts. The bottom line is for expirations at least two months away. We found that all the returns were muted when we extended the expiration dates further, with positive returns being less positive and negative returns being less negative. Extending the expiration dates translated to a smaller decrease in implied volatility, so price swings of the options were less pronounced. For instance, the average returns for long puts at least two months from expiration were –2.81%, while they were –4.46% for the near-month options. The median return was much less negative for the further-away contract as well (–8.97% versus –18.85%). Extending the expiration dates also made the long put positions more likely to be profitable: 40.7% of all long put trades with further expiration dates were profitable, compared to 37.8% of all such trades for the baseline case. Less pronounced time decay also contributes to the higher returns of options with further expiration dates.

Table 5.5 Performance of Long Puts: Further Expiration Dates

Expiration Date	Mean	Minimum	1st Quartile	Median	3rd Quartile	Maximum
Near Month	–4.46%	–99.48%	–53.81%	–18.85%	26.87%	657.10%
Further Month	–2.81%	–99.32%	–33.33%	–8.97%	18.87%	382.30%

Table 5.6 shows similar evidence for the short call strategy. Shorting calls with further expiration dates resulted in slightly better average returns than the baseline case (–4.75% versus –5.00%), but much worse median returns (3.27% versus 12.01%). Only 52.5% of the short calls were profitable when the expiration dates were extended, compared to 55.8% profitable trades for the baseline short call case. Overall, the returns were muted for options with further expiration dates—positive returns were less positive, and negative returns were less negative. In the short call case, larger time decay was likely to contribute to better results for the baseline case.

Table 5.6 Performance of Short Calls: Further Expiration Dates

Expiration Date	Mean	Minimum	1st Quartile	Median	3rd Quartile	Maximum
Near Month	–5.00%	–1041.20%	–41.80%	12.01%	52.21%	99.14%
Further Month	–4.75%	–363.30%	–31.44%	3.27%	31.97%	97.69%

Increasing the Holding Period

We next stretched the holding period of the baseline trades from two days to five days. In the baseline tests, we held options for two days, entering at the closing price one day before the earnings announcement and exiting at the closing price one day after the announcement. We now assume that we exit at the closing price four days after the announcement, creating a five-day holding period. This allowed the option strategies to capture any price drift (i.e., incomplete market reactions), but the larger time decay acted as head winds for the long positions and as tail winds for the short positions.

Table 5.7 shows that when the holding period was two days, the average return for the long put strategy was –6.77%. Extending the holding period for three more days resulted in a substantial decrease in returns: The average return was –10.12% for the five-day holding period. The median and 1st Quartile returns were also much worse for the five-day holding period, suggesting that both time decay and price drift were taking tolls on the long put positions. The hit ratio (percentage of profitable trades) for the long put strategy dropped from 37.8% for the two-day holding period to 34.71% for the five-day holding period. However, when the bets were correct, extending the holding period seemed to be worth the effort, as the 3rd Quartile return was 26.87% for the five-day holding period, higher than the 23.73% return for the two-day holding period. The maximum return was also higher when the holding period was extended (768.70% versus 596.80%). A likely explanation for the results in the right tail of the returns distribution is that the put options were in-the-money, so time decay was muted and price drift dominated.

Table 5.7 Performance of Long Puts: Longer Holding Period

Holding Period	Mean	Minimum	1st Quartile	Median	3rd Quartile	Maximum
Two Days	−6.77%	−99.48%	−52.78%	−18.89%	23.73%	596.80%
Five Days	−10.12%	−99.48%	−68.27%	−30.85%	26.87%	768.70%

Next, we extended the holding period for the short call strategy. The results are presented in Table 5.8. We see a reversal of the pattern observed in the long put strategy. The average return of the short call strategy improved from −6.33% to −2.83% when the holding period was extended from two days to five days. In fact, the five-day holding period had better performance than the two-day holding period all along the returns distribution, as evidenced by the higher 1st Quartile, median, and 3rd Quartile returns for the five-day holding period. Extending the holding period to five days resulted in 59.2% of all trades being profitable, which is higher than the 55.8% hit ratio for the two-day holding period. Both price drift and time decay explain the improved performance for the short call strategy with extended holding period.

Table 5.8 Performance of Short Calls: Longer Holding Period

Holding Period	Mean	Minimum	1st Quartile	Median	3rd Quartile	Maximum
Two Days	–6.33%	–1041.10%	–41.98%	10.00%	48.03%	99.14%
Five Days	–2.83%	–913.75%	–45.30%	22.22%	65.34%	99.31%

Thought Experiment: Knowing Earnings Announcement Returns

We next examined performance of the long put and short call strategies conditioned on the *ex-post* earnings announcement returns. This is not an implementable strategy. Rather, the results in this section help you gauge the *potential* profitability of your trades given realized earnings announcement returns. Understanding the potential profitability helps you better manage the risk of each trade you take on.

To perform this analysis, we sorted all the observations and assigned them into ten equal-size decile portfolios based on earnings announcement returns. By construction, earnings announcement returns were most negative in Decile 1 and most positive in Decile 10. We then examined the distribution of the options' returns in each of these ten portfolios. Here, we are interested in the potential gain or loss of the long put or short call strategy when the earnings announcement return falls into a certain range, say –2% to –3%.

Figure 5.3 shows the long put option returns based on these ranked portfolios. We report the data in more detail in Table A5.3 in the "Appendix" section. The labels of the (horizontal) X-axis in Figure 5.3 show the range of equity earnings announcement returns for each decile portfolio. For example, for Decile 1, all returns are less than –9%. For Decile 10, all returns are greater than 10%. As expected, the returns to the long put trades decrease with the earnings announcement returns. For example, the mean (median) return of the long put strategy is 127.13% (105.74%) for Decile 1, whereas it is –75.70% (–78.88%) for Decile 10.

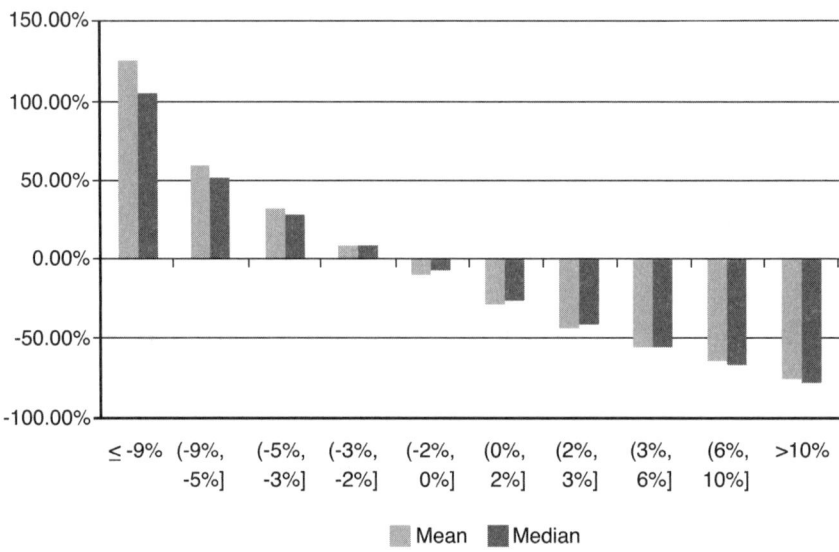

Figure 5.3 Performance of long put options by earnings announcement returns.

Perusing the ranked portfolios, long put strategies were strongly profitable for the first three deciles. They turned a bit riskier in the fourth decile, where all earnings announcement returns were between –3% and –2%. The average long put strategy was still profitable at 9.98% and the median was positive as well at 8.51%. But a significant portion of the trades in this portfolio lost money: More than 25% of the trades had returns less than –2.13%. The most interesting observation is in Decile 5, where earnings announcement returns were still negative (between –2% and 0%). Contrary to the belief that long put positions profit from *any* negative price movement, the average return was *negative* (–10.20%) for this group. In fact, more than 75% of the trades in this group had negative returns, as evidenced by the 3rd Quartile return of –2.17%. Both time decay and the volatility collapse after earnings announcements explain these counterintuitive results. The results highlight the critical differences between the option market and the equity market. Overall, the results suggest that earnings announcement (equity) returns in the range of approximately –3% to –4% is the threshold where a long put position will be profitable. Earnings announcement returns higher than this threshold, even if they are negative, do not necessarily guarantee a winning long put position.

The graph also provides a general sense of how much gain or loss you should expect given the realized earnings announcement return. Take the third and seventh deciles as examples. If the earnings announcement return was somewhere between –5% and –3% (Decile 3), the average gain for the long put trades was 32.71% for two days. On the other hand, if the earnings announcement return was between 3% and 6%, the average loss in two days was –56.56%.

If you consider only the trades for which the underlying equity returns were negative, buying puts was profitable 76.5% of the time. Perhaps the real surprise here is that 23.5% of the long put trades were losing even if you correctly forecast the sign of the earnings announcement return. If the earnings announcement return was positive, there was almost no exception that a long put trade lost money.

We performed a similar analysis for the short call strategy and present the results in Figure 5.4. Detailed data for Figure 5.4 are provided in Table A5.4 in the "Appendix" section. As expected, the mean returns of the short call strategy increased with earnings announcement returns. While the average returns were negative in six deciles for the long put strategy, the average returns were positive in six deciles for the short call strategy. The short call strategy did very well for the first four deciles. The sharp contrast in performance between the long put and the short call strategies was most salient in Deciles 5 and 6. In Decile 5, where equity returns ranged from –2% to 0%, the mean returns from the short call strategy were 22.04%; the median returns were 19.58%; and even the 1st Quartile was a winner at 11.38%. The mean, median, and 1st Quartile returns for the long put strategy in this decile were −10.20%, −8.52%, and −18.18%, respectively. These differences are stunning, given that these trades were for the same underlying stocks, over the same time, and expressing the same views. More surprisingly, the short call strategy had a *positive* average return of 1.46% in Decile 6, where all earnings announcement returns were actually positive. Meanwhile, the long put strategy experienced a blood bath in the same decile, losing 29.43% on average. Volatility collapse after earnings announcements and time decay explain the differences in performance between the two strategies.

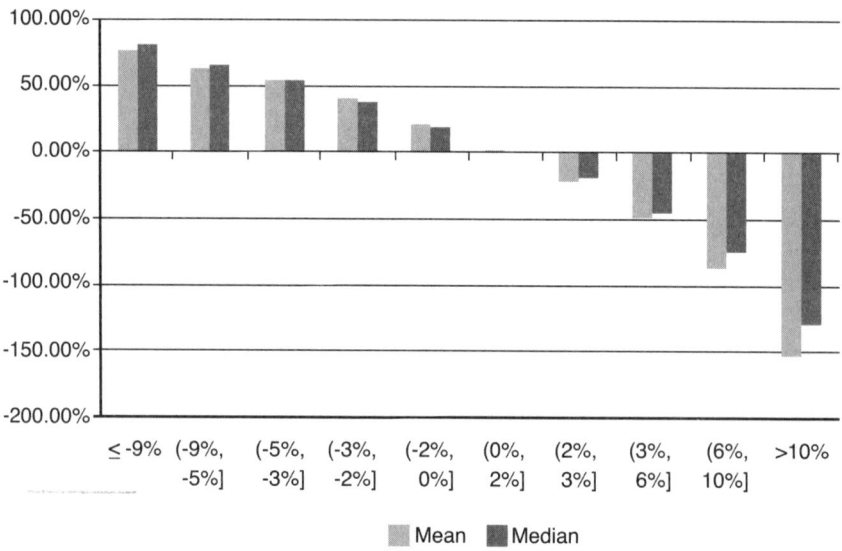

Figure 5.4 Performance of short calls by earnings announcement returns.

Unless the earnings announcement returns are at the extremes (Decile 1 and Decile 10), average and median returns are always higher for the short call strategy than for the long put strategy. Compare the third and seventh deciles as examples to see how much you can gain or lose if earnings announcement returns fall into the ranges defining the two deciles. The average gain for the short call trades was 52.57% when earnings announcement returns were between –5% and –3% (Decile 3), relative to the 32.71% return for the long put strategy. When earnings announcement returns were between 3% and 6% (Decile 7), the average loss was –50.38% for the short call strategy versus –56.56% for the long put strategy.

The evidence suggests that in general shorting calls is a preferred method to express bearish views over buying puts, because both volatility collapse after earnings announcements and time decay work for shorting calls and against buying puts.

The Takeaway

Even when mid-price execution is assumed, the average returns of both the long put and short call strategies are negative. This is in contrast to the small positive average returns of the bullish trades (discussed in the prior chapter). When more conservative entry/exit prices are assumed (i.e., the 75% rule and the worst-price), the mean returns of both strategies turn even more negative, as expected. These results suggest that it is generally unwise to be persistently bearish about earnings announcements, even when you make the most optimistic assumptions about bid-ask spreads.

Similar to the preceding chapter, the median return of the long put strategy is persistently negative, while the median return of the short call strategy is persistently positive, as evidenced by the time-series analysis. As a result, the hit ratio of the short call strategy is significantly higher than that of the long put strategy.

The results of the sensitivity analysis here are comparable to those of the bullish directional trades in the prior chapter. Focusing on the median returns, which are not affected by extreme scenarios, replacing near-the-money strike prices with out-of-the-money strike prices exacerbates the losses from long puts, but improves the profitability of short calls. Extending the expiration date makes the performance of the long puts and short calls less dramatic. Increasing the holding period is unfavorable for long puts, but favorable for short calls. The different impact of time decay on the two strategies contributes greatly to this result.

Contrary to the conventional wisdom that bearish directional trades make money when earnings announcement returns are negative and lose money when they are positive, we find that (1) long puts actually lose money on average when earnings announcement returns are slightly negative (between −2% and 0%) and (2) short calls are on average profitable when earnings announcement returns are slightly positive (between 0% and 2%). At first blush, these results may be counterintuitive, but they are perfectly consistent with what we find in the preceding chapter and highlight the importance of time decay in options trading.

Because of the different risk/return profiles, it is psychologically more appealing to express bearish views through long puts instead of short calls. The evidence in this chapter, however, points in the other direction. Volatility collapse after earnings announcements and time decay were both head winds for the long put strategy but tail winds for the short call strategy. In fact, we conclude from the results of the preceding chapter and this chapter that, from a hit-ratio perspective, it is always better to express your views with a short position than a long position. Of course, the biggest risk to the short positions is the tail risk inherent in the occasional large price movement. To manage tail risk, a diversified portfolio and better security selection are needed.

Endnotes

1. The baseline results in Table 5.3 are different from those in Table 5.1. This is because in Table 5.3 we require options to have both a near-the-money strike and an out-of-the-money

strike, so the sample in Table 5.3 is a subset of the sample in Table 5.1. This will be the case for all remaining tables in this chapter.

Appendix

Table A5.1 Annual Performance of the Long Call Strategy

Year	Mean	1st Quartile	Median	3rd Quartile
1996	–1.67%	–55.08%	–14.09%	24.71%
1997	–3.59%	–44.85%	–13.95%	21.13%
1998	–5.14%	–47.30%	–20.08%	21.85%
1999	1.29%	–42.33%	–8.71%	30.33%
2000	3.20%	–45.45%	–10.32%	32.73%
2001	–7.27%	–45.05%	–15.85%	18.64%
2002	–0.80%	–45.05%	–17.47%	28.48%
2003	–7.40%	–53.85%	–21.54%	21.76%
2004	–3.56%	–59.24%	–20.93%	28.81%
2005	–14.70%	–67.80%	–33.51%	13.81%
2006	–2.57%	–62.41%	–19.34%	38.89%
2007	–6.14%	–62.04%	–21.66%	28.16%
2008	–8.01%	–59.74%	–23.19%	23.33%
2009	–9.96%	–56.66%	–22.14%	23.40%

Table A5.2 Annual Performance of the Short Put Strategy

Year	Mean	1st Quartile	Median	3rd Quartile
1996	–5.07%	–40.65%	10.06%	41.51%
1997	–4.35%	–36.05%	8.20%	39.85%
1998	–7.14%	–40.05%	6.03%	39.09%
1999	–7.54%	–39.11%	8.87%	42.86%
2000	–5.00%	–41.58%	9.52%	46.34%
2001	–9.40%	–43.71%	4.30%	37.06%
2002	–6.37%	–40.12%	2.99%	43.90%

Year	Mean	1st Quartile	Median	3rd Quartile
2003	−8.38%	−41.36%	6.67%	44.02%
2004	−9.68%	−50.00%	7.06%	54.12%
2005	−13.84%	−51.41%	1.33%	53.69%
2006	−1.15%	−38.91%	23.19%	65.32%
2007	−4.10%	−45.55%	20.69%	60.55%
2008	−0.86%	−40.76%	15.12%	56.92%
2009	−4.13%	−42.02%	15.96%	55.73%

Table A5.3 Performance of Long Calls by Earnings Announcement Returns

Earnings Announcement Returns	Mean	1st Quartile	Median	3rd Quartile
≤ −9%	127.13%	67.10%	105.74%	163.72%
(−9%, −5%]	61.10%	30.52%	53.54%	80.00%
(−5%, −3%]	32.71%	13.95%	28.75%	46.73%
(−3%, −2%]	9.98%	−2.13%	8.51%	20.69%
(−2%, 0%]	−10.20%	−18.18%	−8.52%	−2.17%
(0%, 2%]	−29.43%	−36.92%	−26.95%	−19.09%
(2%, 3%]	−43.47%	−53.33%	−41.86%	−31.68%
(3%, 6%]	−56.56%	−68.45%	−56.35%	−43.97%
(6%, 10%]	−65.66%	−78.06%	−67.24%	−53.38%
> 10%	−75.70%	−88.30%	−78.88%	−65.22%

Table A5.4 Performance of Short Puts by Earnings Announcement Returns

Earnings Announcement Returns	Mean	1st Quartile	Median	3rd Quartile
≤ −9%	77.14%	67.35%	80.91%	89.44%
(−9%, −5%]	63.16%	50.00%	64.43%	77.69%
(−5%, −3%]	52.57%	40.29%	52.85%	63.93%
(−3%, −2%]	40.15%	27.85%	38.17%	50.94%
(−2%, 0%]	22.04%	11.38%	19.58%	30.53%
(0%, 2%]	1.46%	−7.63%	0.00%	9.59%

Earnings Announcement Returns	Mean	1st Quartile	Median	3rd Quartile
(2%, 3%]	−22.38%	−32.93%	−19.94%	−8.70%
(3%, 6%]	−50.38%	−66.25%	−45.29%	−28.05%
(6%, 10%]	−88.00%	−110.77%	−75.70%	−51.30%
> 10%	−153.31%	−189.43%	−130.65%	−92.63%

6

Long Volatility Trades

Earnings announcement returns are extremely difficult to forecast, making directional bets risky. Will the stock price spike up 5%? Or will it tank 5%? However, with the help of options, you can trade corporate earnings news without having to guess whether the news will be good or bad. Such strategies, straddles or strangles, involve simultaneously buying or short selling calls and puts of the same stock. Whether the earnings announcement returns are positive or negative, the returns will be favorable to one leg of the trade and unfavorable to the other, so the direction does not matter much. Instead, the profitability of straddles and strangles depends on the degree or magnitude of price changes (not the direction *per se*).

A long straddle or strangle that involves a simultaneous position in a long call and long put, is profitable if the increase in either option's price more than offsets the decrease in the other option's price. This will happen if the price of the underlying equity experiences a large move. Alternatively, a long straddle or strangle can be profitable if both options' prices increase (though this is less common), which can occur if both option premiums increase due to some increased uncertainty (i.e., increased implied volatility). Buyers of straddles and strangles expect volatility to spike, making them long volatility trades.

The rationale for the short straddle or strangle strategy is exactly the opposite. A short straddle or strangle involves simultaneously shorting a call and a put, and is profitable if (1) the decrease in one option's price more than offsets the increase in the other option's price or (2) both options' prices decrease. This happens if the underlying equity return is muted or implied volatility decreases due to the resolution of uncertainty; time decay will also reduce the value of both options. Hence, sellers of straddles and strangles expect volatility to fall, making them short volatility trades.

This chapter describes two basic long volatility trades: long straddles and long strangles. As with prior chapters, we start with the baseline case and present annual results. We then test the sensitivity of long straddles and strangles with respect to different expiration dates and holding periods. Lastly, we analyze the performance of the long straddles and strangles conditional on absolute earnings announcement returns.

Note that our sample selection criteria are different from those in the prior two chapters because volatility trades involve two options while the directional trades we examined involved only one option. In this chapter, we include only options meeting the following liquidity requirements: (1) the bid-ask spread of a straddle/strangle is no more than 10% of the mid-price; (2) the bid price of the straddle/strangle is no smaller than $0.60. The two requirements ensure that bid-ask spreads and transaction costs do not take large tolls on the strategies' profits.

Long Straddles: The Baseline Case

Table 6.1 shows the results of the baseline case of long straddles, which have equal positions in calls and puts of the same strike prices and with the same expiration dates. We continue to use the same standard criteria for this analysis. The strike price is the at-the-money or near-the-money strike (i.e., less than 5% away from the underlying stock price), and the expiration month is the nearest month. We enter into the straddle at the closing prices one day before earnings are announced, and exit the position at the close one day after the earnings announcement, translating into a two-day holding period. To test the sensitivity of the performance of the long straddles to different execution assumptions, we present results based on three bid-ask spread assumptions: the mid-price, the 75% rule, and the worst-price. Comparisons among the three assumptions highlight the importance of controlling for bid-ask spreads in real trading.

Table 6.1 Performance of Long Straddles: The Baseline Case

Execution Assumption	Mean	Minimum	1st Quartile	Median	3rd Quartile	Maximum
Mid-Price	0.00%	−74.22%	−15.85%	−5.56%	8.51%	302.61%
75% Rule	−3.68%	−75.95%	−19.02%	−9.11%	4.56%	290.99%
Worst-Price	−7.24%	−78.13%	−22.22%	−12.50%	0.85%	279.66%

When the mid-price is assumed, the average return of the long straddle is zero. When more conservative execution prices are assumed, the strategy's average return is negative: −3.68% for the 75% rule and −7.24% for the worst-price. On average, long straddle positions are not winning strategies. The median returns are consistently negative, ranging from −5.56% for the mid-price to −12.50% for the worst-price. Assuming the 75% rule, about 30.7% of long straddles are profitable. These results might not be surprising given that buying calls or puts individually (i.e., in isolation) is generally a money-losing strategy. Besides the head winds of volatility collapse and time decay, roughly 50% of earnings announcements have absolute returns less than 2.5%. The evidence suggests that *blindly buying straddles* is unprofitable and that careful security selection is the key to the success of long straddles. Careful security selection can include considerations for such things as growth expectations, separate analysis of revenue and expense surprises, the time-series persistence of earnings surprises, among others.

Long Strangles: The Baseline Case

Strangles are similar to straddles, except that the strike prices of the call and the put are different. Typically, these strike prices are out-of-the-money; that is, the call's strike price is higher than the underlying equity price, and the put's strike price is lower than the underlying equity price. For instance, if a stock is trading at $22.50, a long strangle would consist of a long put with $20 strike and a long call with $25 strike. We require the strike prices of the strangles to be between 5% and 10% away from the underlying equity price.

Table 6.2 summarizes the results. The performance of long strangles is worse than that of long straddles. Even in the best-case scenario of assuming mid-price execution, the results indicate a small average loss of –1.15% for long strangles, versus the break-even result for long straddles. Assuming the 75% rule, the average return for long strangles was –4.81%, compared to –3.68% for long straddles. The minimum, 1st Quartile, and median returns were also lower for long strangles than for long straddles. Because a strangle typically enters into two positions out-of-the-money, the probability of the underlying stock price moving to a profitable point is much lower. However, when absolute equity returns are very large, long strangles outperform long straddles because they are more leveraged, as evidenced by the higher 3rd Quartile and maximum returns for the long strangles. Some investors prefer to buy strangles because they are cheaper than straddles. However, our analysis shows that the benefit of lower option prices is overwhelmed by the dark side of higher probability and larger magnitude of losses. Only 29.7% of all long strangles were profitable (assuming the 75% rule), slightly less than that for the long straddles (30.7%).

Table 6.2 Performance of Long Strangles: The Baseline Case

Execution Assumption	Mean	Minimum	1st Quartile	Median	3rd Quartile	Maximum
Mid-Price	−1.15%	−91.88%	−25.76%	−9.68%	8.78%	436.83%
75% Rule	−4.81%	−92.98%	−28.95%	−13.19%	5.26%	426.70%
Worst-Price	−8.34%	−94.06%	−31.94%	−16.59%	1.82%	416.86%

Time-Series Analysis

Figure 6.1 shows the annual mean and median returns of long straddles around earnings announcements. Detailed data of the annual returns are available in Table A6.1 in the "Appendix" section at the end of this chapter. Except for 1999 and 2000, mean returns for long straddles were consistently negative. In the best year, 2000, the average return from a long straddle was 1.62%. In its worst year, 2009, the average return was −7.15%. The median returns were negative without exception, so more than half of the long straddles were losing trades regardless of the year examined. Long straddles became less profitable over the years. Comparing the first year in the sample, 1996, with the last year, 2009, the average return of long straddles dropped by more than three percentage points and the median return decreased by four percentage points. The decrease in profitability of long straddles over the years examined happened across the board.

Figure 6.2 shows the annual mean and median returns of long strangles from 1996 to 2009. Detailed data for the figure are available in the "Appendix" section in Table A6.2. Overall, the results for long strangles are similar to those for long straddles. The average returns for long strangles were positive in only 1999 and 2000. The best year was 1999, with an average return of 5.49%. In their worst year, 2008, the average return was −11.91%. Median returns were negative in all years. The downward trend in profitability of long strangles was not as pronounced as that of the long straddles, however.

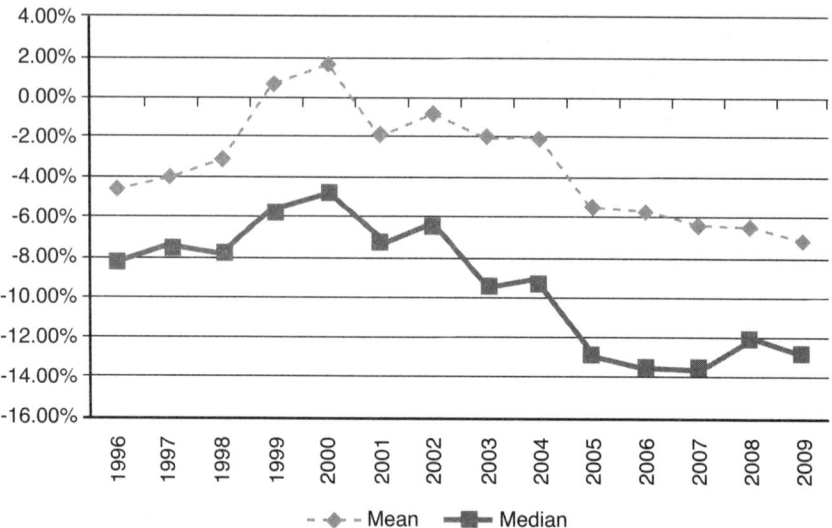

Figure 6.1 Annual performance of long straddles.

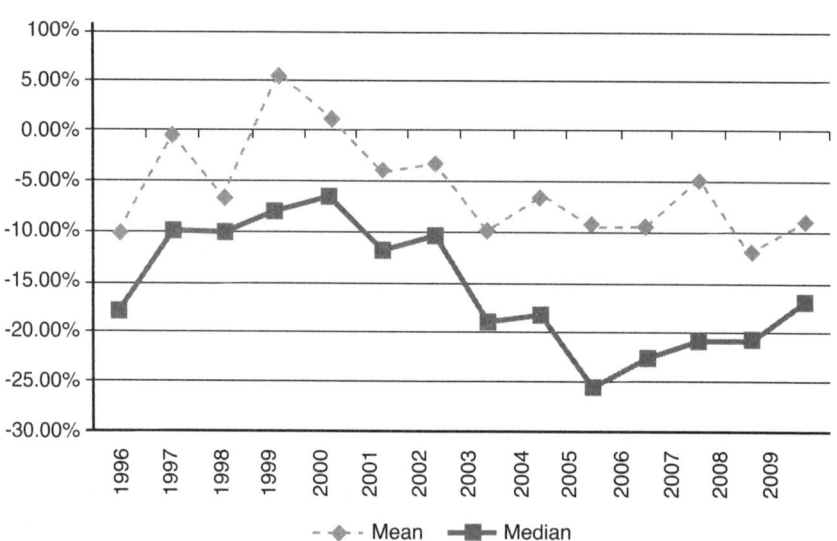

Figure 6.2 Annual performance of long strangles.

Turning the Dials

In the baseline case, we assume that each straddle or strangle was constructed using options with the nearest-month expiration date and held for two days. In the next sections, we examine the impact of extending the expiration date and holding period on performance.

Further Expiration Dates

Table 6.3 summarizes the long straddles assuming that we use an expiration date that is at least two months away from the earnings announcement date. All other aspects of the trades remain unchanged. Only the 75% rule results are shown. We also present the baseline near-month trades for comparison purposes.[1]

Table 6.3 Performance of Long Straddles: Further Expiration Dates

Expiration Date	Mean	Minimum	1st Quartile	Median	3rd Quartile	Maximum
Near Month	–3.57%	–75.95%	–19.13%	–9.28%	4.51%	291.00%
Further Month	–2.05%	–44.94%	–9.95%	–5.16%	1.69%	162.70%

The performance of long straddles improves when further-out expiration months are studied—although they were still on average unprofitable. The mean return was –2.05% for contracts expiring in at least two months compared to the mean return of –3.57% for contracts expiring in the near month. The pattern is similar for the median, as well as the minimum and 1st Quartile returns. However, when earnings announcement returns were very large, extending the expiration date resulted in lower returns. For example, the 3rd Quartile return was 1.69% for contracts expiring in at least two months, versus 4.51% for near-month contracts. Extending expiration dates for long straddles lowered the sensitivity of the strategy to earnings announcement returns. Smaller time decay also benefited the further-out contracts, although the impact was relatively small (because the holding period was only two days). The probability of a profitable trade for long straddles was slightly lower when the expiration dates were extended. Long straddles were profitable 29.1% of the time with further-out expiration dates, compared to 30.7% for the baseline case.

Table 6.4 shows the sensitivity analysis of extending expiration dates for long strangles. The message is very similar to that for the long straddles. Extending the expiration dates lowers long strangles' responses to earnings announcement returns across the distribution. Unlike long straddles, however, the percentage of profitable trades for long strangles increased to 35.0% from 29.7% when the expiration dates were extended.

Table 6.4 Performance of Long Strangles: Further Expiration Dates

Expiration Date	Mean	Minimum	1st Quartile	Median	3rd Quartile	Maximum
Near Month	−3.41%	−92.98%	−27.44%	−12.63%	7.30%	426.70%
Further Month	−1.24%	−43.31%	−10.88%	−4.97%	5.24%	164.20%

Increasing the Holding Period

Next, we examine the impact of extending the holding period. Specifically, we stretched the holding period of the baseline trades from two days to five days. The five-day holding period started at the same time as the baseline (i.e., one day before earnings announcements), but it ended four days (instead of one day) after earnings announcements. Extending the holding period allowed long straddles and strangles to capture potential price drifts that might occur after earnings announcements, but also exposed the trades to more time decay.

The results for long straddles are presented in Table 6.5. The results are consistent with the existence of price drift after earnings announcements. Winning trades (3rd Quartile) became bigger winners. Because long straddles had negative returns on average, extending the holding period increased their losses. In particular, the average return for long straddles was –4.60% for a two-day holding period, and it widened to –8.23% with three extra holding days. The 1st Quartile and median returns were also lower for the five-day holding period, but the 3rd Quartile return was higher for the five-day holding period. Thus, the evidence suggests that it was better to let winning trades run for a few extra days, but losing trades should have been closed immediately.

Table 6.5 Performance of Long Straddles: Longer Holding Period

Holding Period	Mean	Minimum	1st Quartile	Median	3rd Quartile	Maximum
Two Days	–4.60%	–71.75%	–18.60%	–9.30%	2.94%	223.40%
Five Days	–8.23%	–88.92%	–27.61%	–15.62%	3.57%	422.10%

Table 6.6 shows the results for long strangles were similar to those for long straddles. However, although the 3rd Quartile return was positive (2.44%) for the two-day holding period, it became negative (–0.74%) after three extra holding days. The profit from the two-day holding period was quite small, so the time decay of the extra three days can easily push returns into negative territory. Nevertheless, the message remains unchanged: Let the big winners run, but close the losing positions immediately. The recommendation might be counter to your instinct, which psychologists call the "disposition effect." The disposition effect is the psychological preference for taking profits on winning trades but holding onto losing trades, hoping for a reversal of fortune. The evidence in Tables 6.5 and 6.6 shows that the disposition effect can be costly.

Table 6.6 Performance of Long Strangles: Longer Holding Period

Holding Period	Mean	Minimum	1st Quartile	Median	3rd Quartile	Maximum
Two Days	–6.54%	–82.56%	–27.93%	–13.45%	2.44%	426.70%
Five Days	–14.75%	–93.86%	–43.38%	–26.02%	–0.74%	610.80%

Thought Experiment: Knowing Absolute Earnings Announcement Returns

The final set of analyses was based on the thought experiment about how long straddle and strangle strategies would perform if we knew what the absolute earnings announcement returns were going to be ahead of time. With straddles and strangles, we care about the *absolute* instead of *signed* earnings announcement returns because they are volatility trades. The analyses provide you with a quantitative gauge of the potential profitability of the trades. For example, is a 5% earnings announcement return large enough to make a long straddle profitable?

We sort all the observations based on their absolute two-day earnings announcement returns into five equal-size quintile portfolios. Quintile 1 contains the 20% of observations with the smallest absolute market reactions surrounding earnings announcements, and Quintile 5 includes the 20% of observations with the largest absolute earnings announcement returns.

Figure 6.3 illustrates the mean and median long straddle returns for each of the absolute earnings announcement return quintile portfolios. Detailed data are provided in Table A6.3 in the "Appendix" section. As expected, performance of long straddles improved with the absolute earnings announcement returns. The mean return was negative for the first three quintiles, when absolute earnings announcement returns were less than 5.19%. The median returns were negative as well. The percentage of profitable trades (i.e., hit ratio) for the first three quintiles were 2.2%, 10.5%, and 22.2%, respectively. The average was 11.63%, indicating that 88.37% of the time a long straddle strategy lost money when absolute earnings announcement returns were less than 5.19%. Even when absolute earnings announcement returns were between 5.19% and 8.89% (Quintile 4), the average return was barely positive (0.32%) for the long straddle strategy and the median return was negative (−2.84%). This result might seem counterintuitive, because 8% is a fairly large return. However, stocks with such large absolute earnings announcement returns are likely to have a history of volatile market reactions to earnings announcements, and the options market will have factored in this information with expensive option prices (via implied volatility), making it harder for long straddles to become profitable. Long straddles are highly profitable when absolute earnings announcement returns are larger than 8.89% (Quintile 5) with an average return of 25.21% and a median return of 16.67%. In such cases, the magnitude of actual earnings announcement returns was even higher than what the options market predicted.

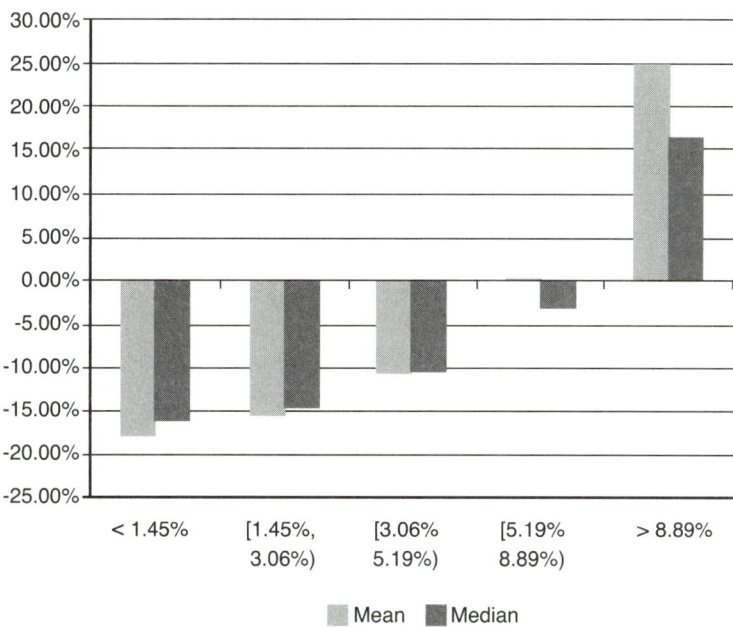

Figure 6.3 Performance of long straddles by absolute earnings announcement returns.

Figure 6.4 shows the performance of long strangles conditional on absolute earnings announcement returns. Detailed data are provided in Table A6.4 in the "Appendix" section. The average returns of long strangles were negative for the first three quintiles when absolute earnings announcement returns were lower than 6.77%. The median returns were negative for the first two quintiles, but turned positive in Quintile 3. The average return became positive for the fourth quintile (2.72%), and the median return was quite large (19.09%). Most of the gains for long strangles came in the last quintile, when absolute earnings announcement returns were larger than 11.40%.

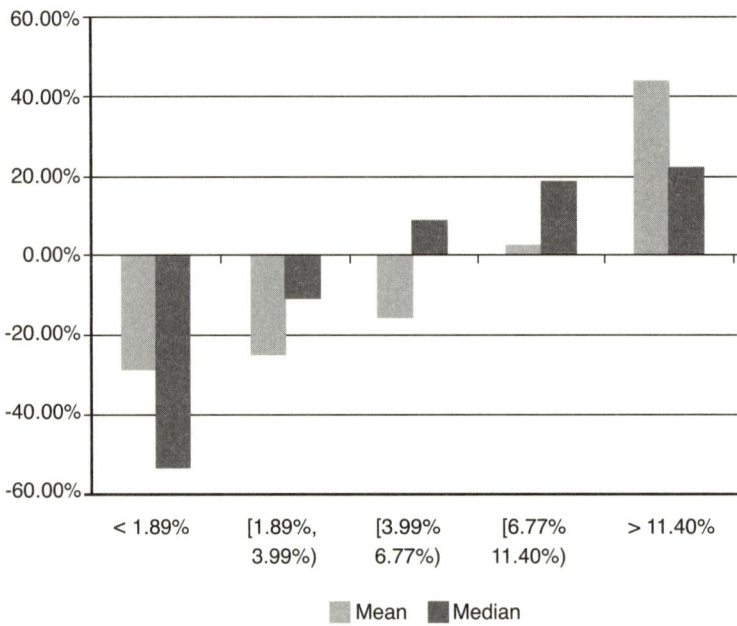

Figure 6.4 Performance of Long strangles by absolute earnings announcement returns.

The Takeaway

Long volatility trades are generally unprofitable even though they occasionally earn outsized returns. Such results are consistent with our analyses of buying calls or puts individually. The odds of profitability are low for long volatility trades: Only about 30% of them are profitable.

Our time-series analysis finds that the average returns of long volatility trades were positive in only two years of the 14-year sample. Median returns were persistently negative, showing that under 50% of trades were positive in all years. There is also some evidence that the profitability of long volatility trades decreased over recent years.

Sensitivity analysis shows that extending expiration dates lessens losses, but increasing the holding period exacerbates losses. However, we also find evidence of price drift after earnings announcements, suggesting that it is beneficial to let winners run for a few extra days but close losing trades immediately.

For both long straddles and strangles, most of the profits came from the top 20% of earnings announcements with the highest absolute earnings announcement returns. In our sample, long straddles turned in solid profits when absolute earnings announcement returns were higher than 9%, while the threshold for long strangles was about 11%.

Endnote

1. As in prior chapters, the baseline results in Table 6.3 differ from those in Table 6.1 because the sample in Table 6.3 is a subset of the sample in Table 6.1.

Appendix

Table A6.1 Annual Performance of Long Straddles

Year	Mean	Median
1996	–4.55%	–8.28%
1997	–3.96%	–7.52%
1998	–3.20%	–7.82%

Year	Mean	Median
1999	0.60%	−5.67%
2000	1.62%	−4.69%
2001	−1.86%	−7.25%
2002	−0.87%	−6.53%
2003	−1.97%	−9.39%
2004	−2.14%	−9.31%
2005	−5.47%	−12.91%
2006	−5.62%	−13.48%
2007	−6.30%	−13.42%
2008	−6.47%	−12.04%
2009	−7.15%	−12.63%

Table A6.2 Annual Performance of Long Strangles

Year	Mean	Median
1996	−9.96%	−17.54%
1997	−0.64%	−9.89%
1998	−6.58%	−10.29%
1999	5.49%	−7.99%
2000	1.34%	−6.50%
2001	−3.97%	−11.79%
2002	−3.38%	−10.55%
2003	−9.82%	−19.12%
2004	−6.59%	−18.29%
2005	−9.19%	−25.22%
2006	−9.35%	−22.78%
2007	−4.87%	−20.83%
2008	−11.91%	−20.75%
2009	−8.98%	−17.00%

Table A6.3 Performance of Long Straddles by Absolute Earnings Announcement Returns

Absolute Earnings Announcement Returns	Mean	Median
< 1.45%	−17.94%	−16.27%
[1.45%, 3.06%)	−15.59%	−14.51%
[3.06%, 5.19%)	−10.41%	−10.68%
[5.19%, 8.89%)	0.32%	−2.84%
> 8.89%	25.21%	16.67%

Table A6.4 Performance of Long Strangles by Absolute Earnings Announcement Returns

Absolute Earnings Announcement Returns	Mean	Median
< 1.89%	−29.65%	−54.00%
[1.89%, 3.99%)	−25.75%	−10.37%
[3.99%, 6.77%)	−16.01%	9.15%
[6.77%, 11.40%)	2.72%	19.09%
> 11.40%	44.64%	22.90%

7

Short Volatility Trades

This chapter examines short volatility trades: short straddles and strangles. Short volatility trades are bets that the underlying stock price will not move substantially (or at least not as much as suggested by the implied volatility embedded in the options). The preceding chapter demonstrated that long volatility trades were profitable only about 30% of the time and profits from the strategies were concentrated in the top 20% of trades with the largest absolute earnings announcement returns. This evidence suggests that shorting volatility might be a more profitable strategy. However, because traders rarely execute trades at the midpoint of the bid-ask spread, the actual performance of short volatility trades is not simply the mirror image or exact opposite of long volatility trades. Unless you are a market maker, you tend to buy close to the ask and sell close to the bid. The round-trip costs can be significant, making profitability far from a sure thing.

The sample used for this chapter is the same sample used in Chapter 6, "Long Volatility Trades," including only those options meeting our liquidity requirements, so the adverse impact from thinly traded options is mitigated beforehand. The rest of the chapter is organized as follows. We first present the baseline (i.e., near-month expiration and two-day holding period) results for short straddles and strangles, as well as their annual performance. Next, we examine the sensitivity of the short volatility strategies with respect to two parameters: the expiration date and the holding period. Lastly, we provide a quantitative gauge of the strategies' profitability conditional on absolute earnings announcement returns.

Short Straddles: The Baseline Case

Table 7.1 presents results of our baseline case for short straddles, which are defined as an equal short position in a put and a call of the same strike price with the same near-month expiration date. The strike price is at-the-money or near-the-money (less than 5% away from the underlying stock price). We enter into the short straddle position at the closing prices one day before earnings are announced, and exit the position at the close one day after the earnings announcement. Similar to prior chapters, we present the performance of the short straddles based on three different execution assumptions: mid-price, the 75% rule, and the worst-price.

Table 7.1 Performance of Short Straddles: The Baseline Case

Execution Assumption	Mean	Minimum	1st Quartile	Median	3rd Quartile	Maximum
Mid-Price	0.00%	–302.61%	–8.51%	5.56%	15.85%	74.22%
75% Rule	–3.83%	–315.38%	–12.63%	1.93%	12.54%	72.40%
Worst-Price	–7.81%	–335.09%	–17.02%	–1.92%	9.28%	70.49%

Performance of the short straddles with mid-price execution should look familiar to you. It is the exact opposite of performance of the long straddles presented in the preceding chapter's Table 6.1. When a trade occurs at the midpoint of the bid-ask spread, the gain on one side of the trade is the same as the loss on the other side. However, most transactions do not occur at the midpoint of the bid-ask spreads, so the gain (loss) of a long position does not equal the loss (gain) of the short position. Specifically, when the 75% rule was applied, the average return of the long straddles was –3.68%. However, with the same execution assumption, the average return of the short straddles was also negative, at –3.83%. The bid-ask spreads take a large toll on the performance of these strategies, and further highlight the importance of examining different execution assumptions.

Focusing on the performance of short straddles, we find that the median return is positive for the 75% rule (1.93%), whereas the median return of *long* straddles for the 75% rule was negative. About 54.9% of short straddles were profitable with the 75% rule, in contrast to the 30.7% hit ratio of the long straddles. The fact that the short straddles have an average return similar to that of the long straddles despite their much higher median return and hit ratio indicates that the occasional large losses have a disproportionate impact on the performance of short straddles. For example, the minimum return for short straddles was –315.38%, more than four times larger than the maximum return of 72.40%.

Short Strangles: The Baseline Case

The performance of short strangles is summarized in Table 7.2. We tested strangles with out-of-the-money options (more than 5% but less than 10% away from the underlying equity price). In general, the results show that short strangles tended to perform better than short straddles. For example, using the 75% rule, the average return of short strangles was –2.65%, compared to –3.83% for short straddles. The median return was much higher for short strangles than for short straddles (6.17% versus 1.93%). Short strangles were profitable 61.2% of the time, compared to 54.9% for short straddles. These results contrast with those in Chapter 6 in which long strangles underperformed long straddles. Long strangles require larger price movements to become profitable relative to long straddles. On the flip side, short strangles can withstand larger price movements relative to short straddles.

The risk of short strangles was in the left tail of earnings announcement returns: When there were losing trades, they were painful. Assuming the 75% rule, more than 25% of the trades lost at least –12.9%, and the maximum loss was –447.26%.

Table 7.2 Performance of Short Strangles: The Baseline Case

Execution Assumption	Mean	Minimum	1st Quartile	Median	3rd Quartile	Maximum
Mid-Price	1.15%	−436.83%	−8.78%	9.68%	25.76%	91.88%
75% Rule	−2.65%	−447.26%	−12.90%	6.17%	22.64%	90.75%
Worst-Price	−6.59%	−458.02%	−17.14%	2.56%	19.59%	89.58%

Time-Series Analysis

Figure 7.1 presents annual mean and median returns of short straddles from 1996 to 2009, assuming the 75% rule. Detailed data are provided in Table A7.1 in the "Appendix" section at the end of this chapter. The average return for short straddles was negative in every year except 2009. However, the median returns were positive for eight years, and were as high as 6.78% (in 2007), showing that more than half of short straddle positions were winners in each of these years. There was a clear upward trend in both the mean and median returns of short straddles since 2000.

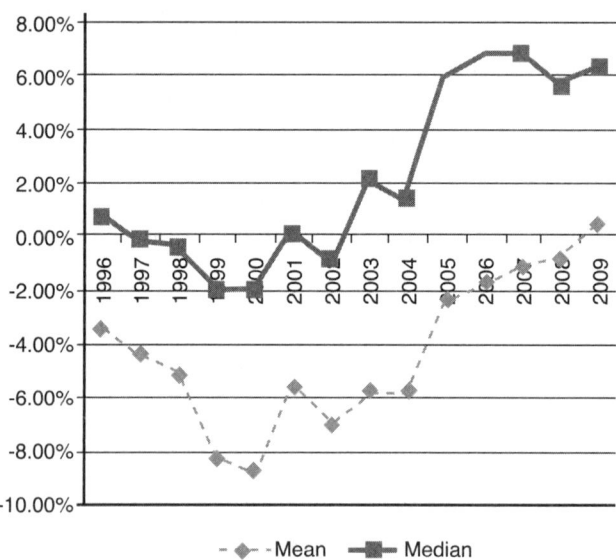

Figure 7.1 Annual performance of short straddles.

An analysis of the short strangles, presented in Figure 7.2, paints a rosier picture (detailed data are available in Table A7.2). Even the mean returns for short strangles were positive in six years (1996, 2003, 2005, 2006, 2008, and 2009). Median returns for short strangles were positive in all years. Median returns were relatively small in years before 2002. For example, they were below 1% in 1999 and 2000. However, since 2003, median returns were above 10% in every year and climbed as high as 18.76% in 2005.

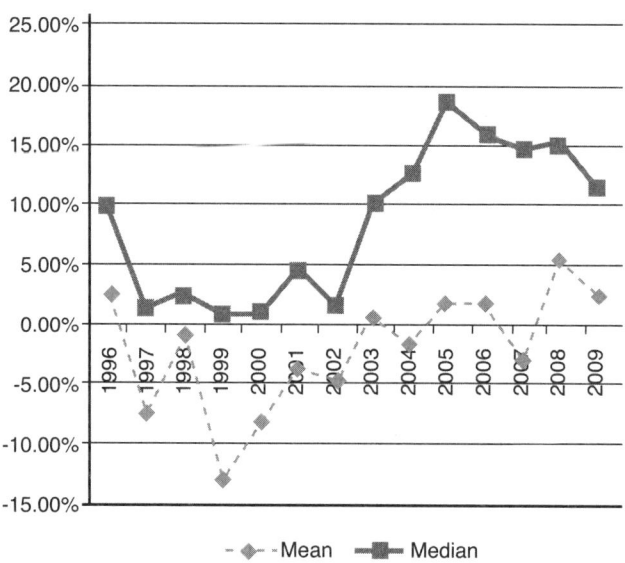

Figure 7.2 Annual performance of short strangles.

Turning the Dials

This section examines how the performance of short volatility trades varies with different expiration dates and holding periods. The baseline case assumed near-month expiration dates and a two-day holding period. We examine how further-out expiration dates (at least two months) and longer holding periods (five-day) affect the results.

Further Expiration Dates

Table 7.3 reexamines short straddles assuming the selection of expiration dates at least two months away from earnings announcements. All other aspects of the trades did not change. We present only the 75% rule results. Results of the default near-month trades are also shown for comparison.[1]

Table 7.3 Performance of Short Straddles: Further Expiration Dates

Expiration Date	Mean	Minimum	1st Quartile	Median	3rd Quartile	Maximum
Near Month	−3.68%	−315.38%	−12.35%	2.28%	12.86%	72.40%
Further Month	−4.12%	−176.92%	−8.04%	−0.74%	4.23%	37.35%

The table shows that performance of short straddles is consistently worse when near-month contracts are replaced with further-out contracts. For instance, the mean return of short straddles was −4.12% for contracts expiring in at least two months compared to the mean return of −3.68% for contracts expiring in the current month. The median return of short straddles turned negative with contracts expiring in at least two months (−0.74%). Extending the expiration dates also lowered the hit ratio for short straddles: 46.4% of the trades were profitable with further-out contracts, compared to 54.9% with near-month contracts. One explanation for the lower profitability is that the benefits of volatility collapse and time decay diminishes with extended expiration dates, resulting in lower returns for short straddles. However, there is a silver lining in extending the expiration dates: When the bets were wrong and earnings announcement returns were unexpectedly large, the loss was smaller for contracts with further-out expiration dates. For example, both the 1st Quartile and minimum returns were better (i.e., smaller losses) for the further-out contracts than for the near-month contracts.

Analysis of short strangles yields similar results. Table 7.4 shows that the average return of short strangles decreased to –4.34% from –3.81% when the expiration dates were extended. The median return was negative as well (–0.46%). Only 48.0% of short strangles were profitable with contracts expiring in at least two months, compared to 61.2% with contracts expiring in the near month. In sum, the evidence suggests that short volatility plays work better when using the nearest-month contracts.

Table 7.4 Performance of Short Strangles: Further Expiration Dates

Expiration Date	Mean	Minimum	1st Quartile	Median	3rd Quartile	Maximum
Near Month	–3.81%	–447.26%	–15.04%	5.77%	21.76%	90.75%
Further Month	–4.34%	–177.23%	–10.78%	–0.46%	5.93%	37.37%

Increasing the Holding Period

Next, we stretch the holding period of the baseline trades from two days to five days. A longer holding period helps short volatility trades by capturing more time decay. Results for short straddles are shown in Table 7.5.

Table 7.5 Performance of Short Straddles: Longer Holding Period

Holding Period	Mean	Minimum	1st Quartile	Median	3rd Quartile	Maximum
Two Days	–2.81%	–242.86%	–11.11%	2.10%	12.16%	67.97%
Five Days	0.96%	–442.67%	–11.49%	8.66%	21.35%	85.75%

As predicted, when we extend the holding period from two days to five days, profitability of short straddles improves significantly. For instance, the average return was –2.81% with a two-day holding period, but with three more holding days, the return turned positive to 0.96%. This is a turnaround of 3.77% in three days. The median short straddle produced a 2.10% return with a two-day holding period, and jumped to 8.66% with three extra holding days. This is a huge improvement on an already great return. There is clear evidence of price drifts as the 1st Quartile results are slightly more negative with the five-day holding period, even with the help of more time decay. However, for short straddles, large price drifts have an adverse impact. The evidence suggests that, similar to the long volatility trades, it is better to let the winners run for a few extra days (note that for short straddles, winners are muted earnings announcement returns), and close losing positions immediately.

Extending the holding period produced even more positive results for short strangles. The results are presented in Table 7.6. The mean return jumped from a small loss (–0.74%) to a large gain (7.82%) with three more holding days. The median returns tripled to 19.85% from 6.46%. Even the 1st Quartile return improved as the loss was almost cut in half (–5.93% versus –10.46%), showing that time decay overwhelms price drifts for short strangles. Overall, the data made a strong case for patience with short volatility trades as time decay works its wonder for option sellers.

Table 7.6 Performance of Short Strangles: Longer Holding Period

Holding Period	Mean	Minimum	1st Quartile	Median	3rd Quartile	Maximum
Two Days	–0.74%	–447.26%	–10.46%	6.46%	21.78%	74.87%
Five Days	7.82%	–650.00%	–5.93%	19.85%	37.73%	93.38%

Thought Experiment: Knowing Absolute Earnings Announcement Returns

In our final analyses, we examine how short volatility trades perform conditional on the *absolute* earnings announcement returns.

This provides you with a sense of the potential profitability of your trades. We first perform the analysis on short straddles and present the results in Figure 7.3. Detailed data are provided in Table A7.3 in the "Appendix" section. Observations are sorted into five equal-size quintile portfolios based on their two-day absolute earnings announcement returns. For example, the bottom quintile (Quintile 1) included the 20% of observations with absolute earnings announcements lower than 1.45%, and the top quintile (Quintile 5) included the 20% of observations with absolute earnings announcement returns higher than 8.89%.

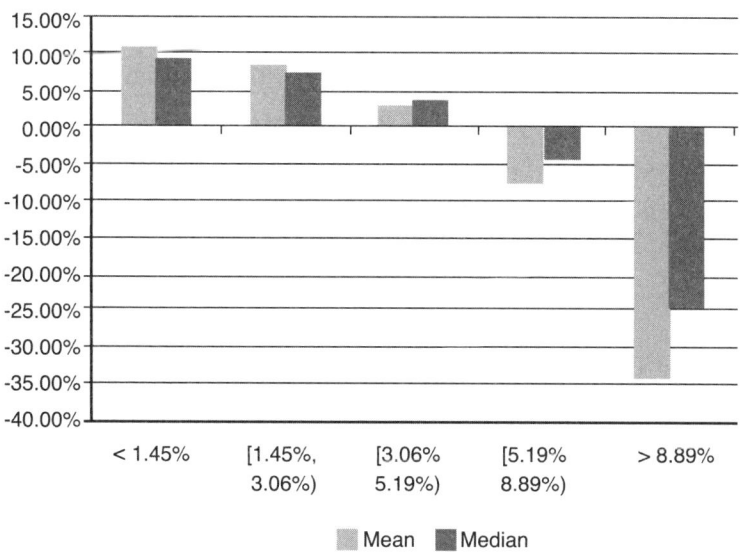

Figure 7.3 Performance of short straddles by absolute earnings announcement returns.

Figure 7.3 presents the mean and median short straddle returns for each of the five absolute earnings announcement return portfolios. Not surprisingly, short straddles perform better with lower absolute earnings announcement returns. Both mean and median returns of short straddles were positive for the first three quintiles, in which absolute earnings announcement returns were lower than 5.19%. The percentages of profitable trades for the three quintile portfolios were 84.4%, 74.7%, and 60.4%, with an average of 73.17%. This number showed that even a 5% move in the stock price amounted to a high likelihood of profitability in short straddles. As the price moves got larger than 5%, the odds started to turn against shorting straddles. In Quintile 4, where underlying absolute stock returns were between 5.19% and 8.89%, the average short-straddle return was negative, at –7.95%. The median return was negative as well (–4.29%), and only 40.0% of the trades were profitable. When stock price reactions were larger than 8.89% (Quintile 5), shorting straddles had large losses, with average (median) returns of –33.91% (–24.62%). However, even in this group, 15.2% of the trades were profitable because the market expected even larger price movements.

Figure 7.4 provides similar evidence for short strangles. Detailed data are provided in Table A7.4 in the "Appendix" section. Short strangles performed very well for the first three quintiles, when absolute earnings announcement returns were lower than 6.77%. Among these three quintiles, the average return was more than 17% and the median return was more than 18%. The hit ratios were very high for the three quintiles, ranging from 92.8% for the first quintile to 70.6% for the third quintile with an average of 83.77%. The short strangles started to lose money when absolute earnings announcement returns were larger than 6.77%. When the absolute earnings announcement returns were between 6.77% and 11.40% (Quintile 4), the average (median) return of short strangles was –10.37% (–4.60%) and the percentage of profitable trades dropped to 42.2%. When absolute earnings announcement returns were larger than 11.40% (Quintile 5), shorting strangles suffered heavy losses, with an average (median) return of –54% (–35%) and a 12.5% hit ratio.

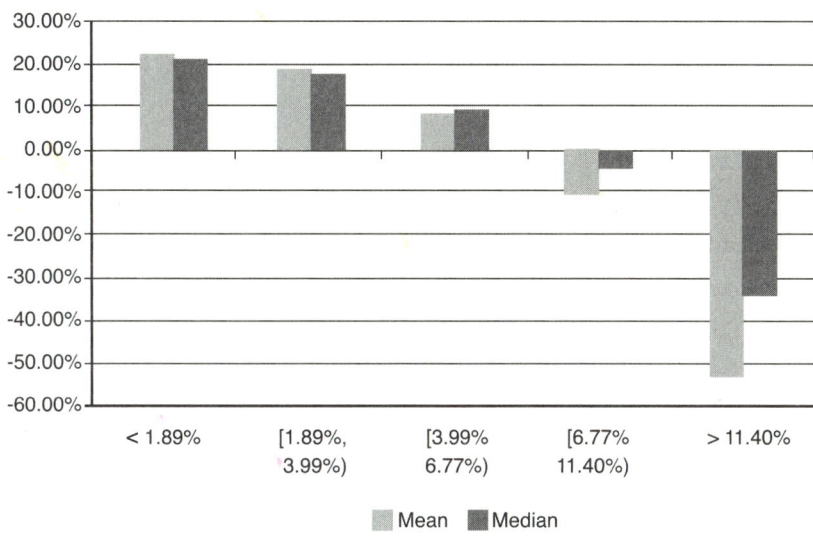

Figure 7.4 Performance of short strangles by absolute earnings announcement returns.

The Takeaway

Shorting volatility indiscriminately, much like buying volatility indiscriminately, is generally unprofitable because of the occasional large losses and fighting against bid-ask spreads. However, the odds of profits are much higher for short volatility trades than for long volatility trades. These results are consistent with those from directional trades: From a hit-ratio perspective, shorting options is more profitable than buying options because short positions benefit from volatility collapse after earnings announcements and from time decay in option values.

The time-series analysis reveals that the average short straddle returns were positive in only one year, but average returns of short strangles were positive in six years. Persistently positive median returns of short strangles suggest that more than 50% of the short strangles were profitable in all sample years. Moreover, the profitability of short volatility trades exhibited a strong upward trend in recent years.

Extending the expiration dates reduced the profitability of short volatility trades, but increasing the holding period greatly improved it primarily due to further time decay. For straddle sellers, it is better to close losing positions immediately, but strangle sellers can hold onto losing positions for a few days to let time decay help recover losses.

In our sample, short straddles were highly profitable when absolute earnings announcement returns were lower than 5%, while short strangles withstood 6% to 7% price movements. However, losses can be steep for short volatility trades when absolute earnings announcement returns are large (roughly 9% for short straddles and 11% for short strangles).

Endnote

1. As before, baseline results in Table 7.3 differ from those in Table 7.1 due to sample differences.

Appendix

Table A7.1 Annual Performance of Short Straddles

Year	Mean	Median
1996	−3.48%	0.60%
1997	−4.35%	−0.15%
1998	−5.10%	−0.41%
1999	−8.24%	−1.91%
2000	−8.76%	−1.99%
2001	−5.52%	0.00%
2002	−6.96%	−0.90%
2003	−5.80%	1.98%

Year	Mean	Median
2004	−5.81%	1.41%
2005	−2.45%	5.88%
2006	−1.78%	6.67%
2007	−1.10%	6.78%
2008	−0.74%	5.60%
2009	0.49%	6.25%

Table A7.2 Annual Performance of Short Strangles

Year	Mean	Median
1996	2.39%	9.42%
1997	−7.63%	1.09%
1998	−1.16%	2.52%
1999	−13.24%	0.72%
2000	−8.43%	0.72%
2001	−3.85%	4.23%
2002	−5.08%	1.49%
2003	0.60%	10.20%
2004	−1.74%	12.50%
2005	1.58%	18.76%
2006	1.49%	15.70%
2007	−2.92%	14.59%
2008	5.18%	15.07%
2009	2.40%	11.57%

Table A7.3 Performance of Short Straddles by Absolute Earnings Announcement Returns

Absolute Earnings Announcement Returns	Mean	Median
< 1.45%	11.00%	9.24%
[1.45%, 3.06%)	8.52%	7.62%
[3.06%, 5.19%)	3.17%	3.82%
[5.19%, 8.89%)	−7.95%	−4.29%
> 8.89%	−33.91%	−24.62%

Table A7.4 Performance of Short Strangles by Absolute Earnings Announcement Returns

Absolute Earnings Announcement Returns	Mean	Median
< 1.89%	22.90%	21.41%
[1.89%, 3.99%)	19.09%	18.31%
[3.99%, 6.77%)	9.15%	9.45%
[6.77%, 11.40%)	−10.37%	−4.60%
> 11.40%	−54.00%	−35.00%

8

Buy Volatility before Earnings Announcements

Chapter 6, "Long Volatility Trades," examined long straddle/strangle trades around earnings announcements. In those trades, straddles/strangles were bought one day before the earnings announcements and closed one day after the announcements. The purpose was to harvest volatility (i.e., large price movements) caused by the information released in earnings announcements. However, a popular strategy among options traders aims to profit from increased volatility *prior to* earnings announcements to avoid direct exposure to the risks related to the announcement itself. The rationale behind the strategy is that uncertainty about the news coming out of earnings announcements intensifies as the announcement date approaches. Investors flock to the options market to either speculate on the news or hedge their positions. Option trading volume typically spikes around earnings announcements. The heightened uncertainty creates higher demand for options and drives up option prices (through implied volatility).

To exploit this predictable increase in options' implied volatility, you can "buy volatility" in the days or weeks prior to the earnings announcements by longing straddles/strangles and close the positions a day before the announcements when implied volatility is at its highest level. The argument is compelling and there are many anecdotal examples of its success, but we want to see empirical, data-driven evidence of its success (or failure). After all, the strategy is not without its challenges. Time decay is a strong and unquestionable head wind to this strategy. This strategy is not expected to benefit from large price movements during the relatively quiet, uneventful holding period because there is no clear catalyst to induce such large price movements (because trades are unwound before the actual announcement). Thus, the profitability of the strategy is primarily determined by the competing forces of increased implied volatility and time decay. A rise in implied volatility during the holding period is likely but not certain, but the time decay is undeniable. For the strategy to be profitable, the rise in implied volatility has to be sufficiently large to offset time decay.

Another challenge with the strategy is that the timing of entry is unclear. Should you establish positions five days before the earnings announcements? How about ten days? If the positions are established too close to the earnings announcement, implied volatility might have already risen substantially, reducing the strategy's profitability. But if the positions are established too early, time decay can cause significant damage.

Although the strategy is very popular, we are not aware of any formal studies on its performance. In this chapter, we use actual options prices to test the strategy and its sensitivity to various factors.

Buying Volatility before Earnings Announcements: The Baseline Case

The baseline case to exploit the run-up in implied volatility prior to earnings announcements is as follows: You enter long straddle positions five days before each earnings announcement, and exit the positions one day before the announcement, creating a five-day holding period. The option contracts expire in the nearest month. To simulate real trading, the strike price of the straddle is required to be within 5% of the closing price of the stock six days before earnings announcements (that is, the day before the position is entered). Three different bid-ask spread assumptions are used: the mid-price, the 75% rule, and the worst-price. The results are presented in Table 8.1.

Table 8.1 Performance of Long Volatility before Earnings Announcements: The Baseline Case

Execution Assumption	Mean	Minimum	1st Quartile	Median	3rd Quartile	Maximum
Mid-Price	–0.45%	–82.22%	–13.54%	–4.86%	8.10%	407.20%
75% Rule	–4.12%	–83.70%	–16.94%	–8.49%	4.12%	398.88%
Worst-Price	–7.66%	–85.11%	–20.10%	–11.80%	0.00%	390.74%

On average, buying volatility before earnings announcements was unprofitable, even assuming the optimistic mid-price execution prices. The average return was negative, –0.45%, and the median return was more negative, –4.86%, indicating that less than 50% of trades were profitable. Results were even less appealing when considering more realistic execution assumptions. For example, using the 75% rule, the mean return was –4.12% and the median return was –8.49%. There were certainly winners among the strategy: A quarter of the trades returned more than 4.12% and the maximum return was close to 400%. Assuming the 75% rule, only 31.55% of the trades were profitable. These returns were comparable to returns of the long volatility trades around earnings announcements. Overall, this outcome casts doubt on the validity of this strategy.

Time Series Analysis

Figure 8.1 shows annual mean and median returns of the long straddles during the five days before earnings announcements, assuming the 75% rule. Detailed data of the annual returns are included in the "Appendix" section at the end of this chapter (Table A8.1). The results are disheartening for supporters of the strategy. The mean returns were negative in all years examined. In the best year, 1997, the average return was –0.79%. In its worst year, 2001, the average return was –11.14%. The median returns were also negative without exception, so more than half of the long straddles were unprofitable in every year studied. There was no clear trend in the performance of the strategy over the years. The strategy's performance worsened in the late 1990s and bottomed out in 2001. It then rebounded until 2007 and took a dive in the last two years to about the long-term average.

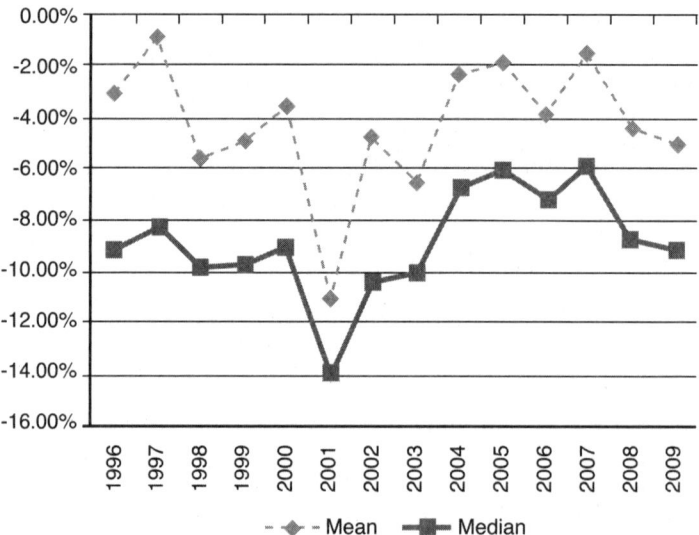

Figure 8.1 Annual performance of long volatility before earnings announcements.

Turning the Dials

In this section, we examine the sensitivity of the performance of the strategy with respect to two parameters: expiration date and holding period. The baseline case assumed the near-month expiration date and a five-day holding period. In the sensitivity tests, the expiration date is extended to at least two months away from the trading day; and the five-day holding period is extended to ten days.

Further Expiration Dates

Table 8.2 summarizes the performance of long straddles before earnings announcements using option contracts with different expiration dates. Option contracts with farther out expiration dates experience less time decay than option contracts with the near-month expiration because further out contracts have lower theta. All other aspects of the trades remain the same. The 75% rule is assumed and baseline results are also presented for comparison purposes.[1]

Table 8.2 Performance of Long Straddles before Earnings Announcements: Further Expiration Dates

Expiration Date	Mean	Minimum	1st Quartile	Median	3rd Quartile	Maximum
Near Month	−4.19%	−67.34%	−16.75%	−8.38%	4.01%	398.88%
Further Month	−2.73%	−30.68%	−8.90%	−4.53%	1.23%	110.56%

Using a later expiration date does not change the tenor of these results. Performance of long straddles before earnings announcements improved when expiration dates were extended. However, the strategy was still unprofitable, albeit less so than the baseline case. The mean return of the strategy with contracts expiring in at least two months was −2.73%, compared with the mean return of −4.19% for contracts expiring in the near month. The pattern was similar for the median return as well as the minimum and 1st Quartile returns. The median return for the two-month-out expiration contracts was −4.53%, relative to the −8.38% for the nearest-month expirations. The improved (though still negative) performance was due to time decay being a less powerful force in further-out contracts than in near-month contracts.

On the other hand, when the strategy pays off, extending the expiration date results in lower returns. For example, the 3rd Quartile return was 1.23% for contracts with further-out expiration contracts, versus 4.01% for contracts with the near-month expiration dates. Although long straddles with further-out expiration contracts had higher mean and median returns, their hit ratio was lower than that of near-month expiration contracts. With near-month expiration contracts, 31.23% of the trades were profitable. That number dropped to 29.56% with further-out contracts.

Increasing the Holding Period (or Entering the Position Earlier)

Next, we test the strategy by entering into positions earlier. In the baseline case, straddles were established five trading days before earnings announcements. We now consider entering the positions ten days before earnings announcements, which is about two calendar weeks. The exit date was the same for both strategies, the day before the announcement. This setup allowed for the possibility that increased implied volatility occurred earlier than five days before the announcement. A countervailing force was that time decay became a greater concern with the holding period extended to ten days. Which force would dominate is an empirical question.

The results are presented in Table 8.3. Performance deteriorated markedly when positions were established ten days instead of five days prior to earnings announcements. Average returns dropped to –8.31% for the ten-day holding period from –2.84% for the five-day holding period. Median returns were much worse: –13.77% for the ten-day holding period versus –7.32% for the five-day holding period. The ten-day holding period results were worse than the five-day holding period at almost all points on the return distribution except for a slightly higher maximum return. The hit ratio turned significantly lower with early entry as well. When positions were established five days prior to earnings announcements, 34.95% of trades were profitable. The percentage dropped to 28.26% when positions were established ten days ahead of earnings announcements.

Because time decay has a negative impact on long straddles' performance, possible explanations for the results are that either (1) the rise in implied volatility was nonexistent in the extra five holding days (i.e., from ten days prior to earnings announcements to five days prior) or (2) the rise in implied volatility was too small to offset the negative impact of time decay. Either way, time decay dominated the rise in implied volatility, making earlier entry timing a worse choice. The results are also consistent with long straddle results around earnings announcements (Chapter 6): For long positions, time decay is a strong head wind to fight off.

Table 8.3 Performance of Long Straddles before Earnings Announcements: Longer Holding Period

Holding Period	Mean	Minimum	1st Quartile	Median	3rd Quartile	Maximum
Five Days	−2.84%	−83.70%	−16.75%	−7.32%	6.18%	223.62%
Ten Days	−8.31%	−87.29%	−25.35%	−13.77%	2.62%	245.15%

Thought Experiment: Knowing Absolute Pre-Earnings Announcement Returns

How would this strategy perform if we knew what the *absolute pre-earnings-announcement* returns were going to be? Because the long volatility strategy was applied to the period before earnings announcements, performance was conditioned on the absolute *pre-earnings announcement* returns. This analysis enhances our understanding of the sources and likely ranges of the profitability of the long volatility before earnings announcement strategy.

We sorted all observations based on absolute five-day pre-earnings announcement returns (from announcement day –5 to announcement day –1) into five equal-size quintile portfolios. Quintile 1 contained the 20% of observations that had the smallest absolute pre-announcement returns, while Quintile 5 included the 20% of observations with the largest absolute pre-announcement returns.

Figure 8.2 summarizes mean and median long-straddle returns for each of the absolute pre-earnings-announcement-return quintile portfolios. Detailed data are provided in Table A8.2 in the "Appendix" section. Several observations emerge from the graph. First, there remains a strong positive association between returns from long straddles and absolute stock returns. Figure 8.2 looks very similar to Figure 6.3. Both graphs document a strong positive relationship between the performance of long straddles and the absolute stock returns during the long straddles' holding period. Second, in the first three quintiles, long straddles *before* earnings announcements had fewer negative returns than long straddles *around* earnings announcements (Figure 6.3) even though the former strategy suffered larger time decay than the latter (five-day versus two-day holding periods). The likely reason for this difference is that the long volatility before earnings announcements strategy was helped by the rise in implied volatility during the holding period, whereas the long volatility around earnings announcements suffered from volatility collapse after the announcements. Third, both mean and median returns were negative for the first four quintiles (80% of the trades), meaning that the strategy frequently incurred losses when absolute pre-announcement returns were less than 7.26%. The percentages of profitable trades for the first four quintiles were 9.0%, 15.6%, 24.9%, and 42.6%, respectively. The average was only 23.03%, indicating that more than three-quarters of the time the trade was a loser. Long straddles had an average return of 14.48% when absolute pre-earnings announcement returns were larger than 7.26% (Quintile 5). The median return was 8.62%.

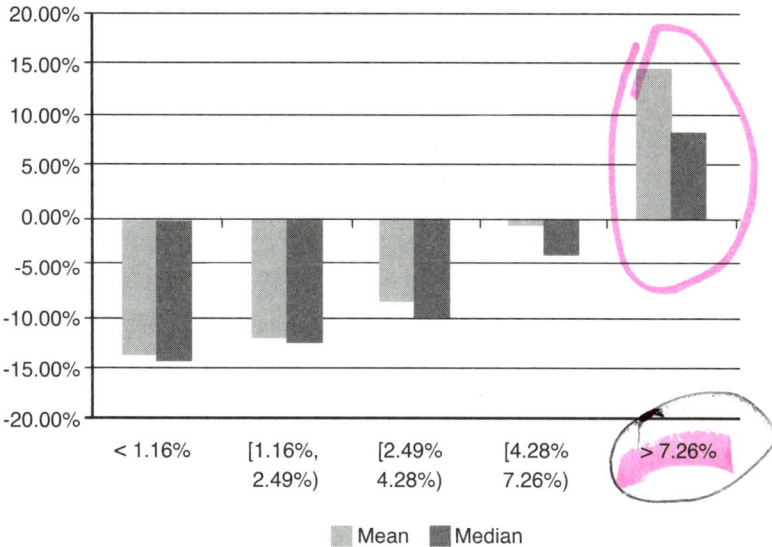

Figure 8.2 Performance of long straddles before earnings announcements by absolute pre-earnings announcement returns.

The Takeaway

Our empirical results challenge the validity of the strategy of buying volatility before earnings announcements. Average returns of the strategy were negative and only about 30% of the trades were profitable.

The time-series analysis showed that average returns of long volatility trades were negative in all 14 years in the sample, and the median returns were worse. There was no sign that the strategy's performance was improving in recent years.

Extending expiration dates lessened losses, as it did to long positions in general. Establishing positions ten days instead of five days ahead of earnings announcements made performance worse. Either there was no appreciable rise in implied volatility during the five extra days or the rise in implied volatility was insufficient to offset the increased time decay.

The average return of the strategy was positive only for the quintile portfolio with the highest absolute pre-announcement returns, in which returns were higher than 7.26%. For the other four quintiles or 80% of the observations, average losses were about –9% and less than a quarter of the trades were profitable.

Endnote

1. Baseline results in Tables 8.1 and 8.2 are different because the sample in Table 8.2 is a subset of the sample in Table 8.1.

Appendix

Table A8.1 Annual Performance of Long Straddles before Earnings Announcements

Year	Mean	Median
1996	–3.00%	–9.12%
1997	–0.79%	–8.34%
1998	–5.54%	–9.89%
1999	–4.95%	–9.73%
2000	–3.66%	–9.06%
2001	–11.14%	–14.04%
2002	–4.79%	–10.47%
2003	–6.48%	–10.16%
2004	–2.22%	–6.68%
2005	–1.85%	–6.11%
2006	–3.87%	–7.12%
2007	–1.48%	–5.86%
2008	–4.47%	–8.77%
2009	–4.99%	–9.12%

Table A8.2 Performance of Long Straddles before Earnings Announcements by Absolute Pre-Earnings Announcement Returns

Absolute Pre-Earnings Announcement Returns	Mean	Median
< 1.16%	−13.79%	−14.17%
[1.16%, 2.49%)	−12.22%	−12.58%
[2.49%, 4.28%)	−8.27%	−9.89%
[4.28%, 7.26%)	−0.79%	−3.70%
> 7.26%	14.48%	8.62%

9

Ride the Post-Earnings-Announcement Drift

The preceding chapter discussed entering positions a week or two prior to earnings announcement dates, to potentially exploit the run-up of implied volatility in the period before anticipated "big news" events. In this chapter, the other side of the timeline is examined. We examine the potential for profits in the period *after* earnings announcement days. A long line of studies in the accounting and finance literature points to a phenomenon known as *"post-earnings-announcement drift,"* or PEAD, which reflects the tendency of stock prices to "drift" (i.e., continue) in the same direction as the initial market reactions to earnings announcements. Specifically, if the market reacts very strongly and positively to a stock's earnings announcement, its price is likely to trade higher, relative to the market, in the following months. Similarly, a stock with a very large negative earnings announcement return is likely to trade lower, relative to the market, in the following months.

What explains the PEAD phenomenon? There are three general theories. The first theory states that PEAD is actually compensation to investors for specific risks, such as liquidity risk and arbitrage risk. The second theory hypothesizes that PEAD reflects the market's underreaction to earnings news; because of the growing complexities in accounting and other information disclosed in earnings announcements, investors can only gradually digest the new information contained in the announcement, and therefore gradually incorporate such information into their valuation of the stock, creating the subsequent drift. The third theory simply states that PEAD does not actually exist. Perhaps the findings arise from erroneous data or incorrect statistical analysis. However, numerous studies with different samples and methodologies all confirm the existence of PEAD, suggesting that PEAD is very real. Perhaps both risks (the first theory) and behavioral bias (the second theory) contribute to PEAD, but the exact reasons are not important. The question is whether PEAD can translate into profitable options trades.

Before we start the analysis, three important issues are worth noting. First, the timing of implementing a PEAD trade is different from that of other strategies. Most strategies are implemented when earnings news is unknown, whereas the PEAD strategy is implemented *after* the news come out. This difference is important because the bulk of the news has already hit the market, so there is no reason to expect implied volatility to rise or decline. Thus, a PEAD trade is not a volatility trade. Second, unlike the directional trades examined in Chapters 4, "Bullish Directional Trades," and 5, "Bearish Directional Trades," where no prediction was made about the direction of stock returns (we left that prediction to you), the PEAD trade is all about predicting which way the stock price will go. And the prediction is straightforward because it assumes *momentum*: It predicts that stocks with large positive earnings announcement returns are likely to drift higher, and stocks with large negative earnings announcement returns are likely to drift lower. Third, in prior chapters, strategies were applied to all options indiscriminately, but in a PEAD trade, different strategies are applied to different options. For example, in the preceding chapter you bought volatility prior to earnings announcements for all stocks because you had no information to determine which ones were more likely to experience a jump in implied volatility during the pre-announcement period. However, in a PEAD trade you apply the bullish directional trades to stocks with *large positive* earnings announcement returns, and implement the bearish directional trades to stocks with *large negative* earnings announcement returns. It is important to note that the PEAD trade is only applied to stocks with sufficiently large earnings announcement returns, which means you do not execute trades in the post-earnings-announcement period to a large number of stocks with relatively small earnings announcement returns.

Post-Earnings-Announcement Drift in Stock Prices

This section examines whether there is PEAD in stocks used in our sample. Our sample is quite different from the sample of other studies because only stocks whose options meet stringent liquidity requirements are included, which makes our sample a small subset of the other studies. Establishing the existence of PEAD for the stocks in this sample is important because the whole option strategy is based on the existence of continuation in price movement. (If no momentum exists in the underlying equity, there's no point in trying to implement PEAD.) The cumulative abnormal stock returns (hereafter CAR) over the two-day window around earnings announcements are used to measure earnings announcement returns. These returns are sorted from low to high. Academic studies usually break samples into quintiles or deciles. This is a sensible approach because it ensures that at any point the sample is divided evenly regardless of the level of earnings announcement returns. There are two drawbacks to this approach, however. First, you need to know the earnings announcement returns of the full universe of publicly-traded stocks to be able to divide the sample into quintiles or deciles, but this information is difficult to obtain. Second, this approach measures relative instead of absolute performance of earnings announcement returns. Even if all stocks have great earnings announcement returns, some will be classified as "bad" news because their earnings announcement returns are lower than those of other stocks. To overcome these two issues, we use intuitive, heuristic earnings announcement return cutoffs. Such cutoffs are more straightforward and can be easily applied without knowing the distribution of earnings announcement returns, and they take into account the level of earnings announcement returns.

Two CAR cutoffs were used: ±5% and ±8%. The ±5% cutoff means that only those stocks whose earnings announcement returns were greater than 5% (good news) or less than –5% (bad news) were included. The ±8% is a more stringent requirement, which included only stocks with earnings announcement returns above 8% or below –8%. Stock prices were tracked in the 22 trading days (about one calendar month) starting from the second day after earnings announcements. This provided a sense of how much momentum a stock had in the month after a big earnings-announcement-related stock price movement.

Table 9.1 presents statistics about the underlying equity stock returns in the month following three different levels of earnings announcement returns, in which the cutoff was ±5%. In the first line of the table, the month-long performances after earnings announcements for all stocks with a –5% or worse earnings announcement returns are summarized. Average returns for these stocks were 0.87%. The next line shows results for stocks with earnings announcement returns between –5% and 5%. For this group, the average return in the month following the announcement was 1.66%, which is 0.79% higher than the previous group. The 0.79% difference was for a month, so the annualized difference was 9.48%. The best performance came from the group experiencing greater than 5% earnings announcement reruns. The average return for this group during the same one-month period was 2.13%, or 1.26% (per month, and 15.12% per year) higher than that of the first group. Median returns, as well as returns on other points of the return distributions, showed the same pattern. Thus, like many samples studied in the past, PEAD was very strong in this sample.

Table 9.1 Post-Earnings-Announcement Drift: ±5% Cutoff

[handwritten note: UNDERLYING EQUITY AFTER ONE MONTH (22 days)]

CAR	Mean	Minimum	1st Quartile	Median	3rd Quartile	Maximum
≤ –5%	0.87%	–90.66%	–8.26%	0.15%	8.78%	262.94%
(–5%, 5%)	1.66%	–84.97%	–4.25%	1.35%	7.16%	218.02%
≥ 5%	2.13%	–82.92%	–5.90%	1.60%	9.25%	323.95%

Table 9.2 shows results for the ±8% cutoff. The results are mostly the same, with average returns of the good and bad news groups being more extreme. The group with earnings announcement returns lower than –8% had average returns of 0.82% in the month following the earnings announcement, lower than the 0.87% return for the group with earnings announcement returns lower than –5%. The group with earnings announcement returns greater than 8% outperformed the group with earnings announcement returns greater than 5% (2.31% versus 2.13%). Although the results are more extreme for the ±8% cutoff, they also suggest that the advantage of targeting more extreme earnings announcement returns diminishes quickly.

Table 9.2 Post-Earnings-Announcement Drift: ±8% Cutoff

CAR	Mean	Minimum	1st Quartile	Median	3rd Quartile	Maximum
≤ –8%	0.82%	–90.66%	–9.45%	0.00%	9.58%	262.94%
(–8%, 8%)	1.61%	–84.97%	–4.55%	1.29%	7.35%	218.02%
≥ 8%	2.31%	–74.62%	–6.64%	1.62%	10.20%	323.95%

Options Strategies for Post-Earnings-Announcement Drift

As discussed earlier, directional options trades should be used to exploit PEAD. Bullish directional trades are applied to stocks with large positive earnings announcement returns, and bearish directional trades are applied to stocks with large negative earnings announcement returns.

Bullish Directional Trades

Table 9.3 shows the distribution of returns from a bullish options strategy after viewing a 5% or greater earnings announcement return. Results from two bullish trades are compared: long calls versus short puts. For both strategies, positions are opened one day *after* earnings announcements and held for 22 trading days. At-the-money or near-the-money strike prices for both the call and the put options were studied. Also, all options had expiration dates at least two months after the positions were established.

Table 9.3 Performance of Bullish Directional Trades after Large Positive Earnings Announcement Returns: ±5% Cutoff

CAR ≥ 5%	Mean	Minimum	1st Quartile	Median	3rd Quartile	Maximum
Long Call	–3.23%	–99.63%	–67.27%	–25.60%	38.59%	701.07%
Short Put	15.60%	–544.27%	–15.92%	34.10%	67.62%	98.39%

On average, the long call strategy was a loser, with –3.23% returns, even though the stock price advanced 2.13% during this period. Median returns were much worse at –25.60%. Because options were purchased after earnings announcements, it is unlikely that volatility collapse accounted for this poor performance. A far more likely explanation is that the time decay dominated the stock price movement. Over the 22-day holding period, time decay was so large that the calls lost significant value despite favorable movement of the underlying equity's stock price. When the stock price spiked, long call positions paid off handsomely, as evidenced by the 701.07% maximum return. However, the statistics are dismal for the long call strategy overall.

On the other hand, the short put strategy performed quite well. The average return was 15.60%, and the median return was 34.10%. Among those short put trades, 68.55% of them were positive, compared to a 38.31% hit ratio for long calls. Both upward stock price movement (PEAD) and time decay helped the short put strategy.

Table 9.4 repeats the analysis of stocks with larger than 8% absolute earnings announcement returns. The results were similar to those in Table 9.3. Again, the short put strategy was a superior choice compared to the long call strategy in exploiting positive PEAD.

Table 9.4 Performance of Bullish Directional Trades after Large Positive Earnings Announcement Returns: ±8% Cutoff

CAR ≥ 8%	Mean	Minimum	1st Quartile	Median	3rd Quartile	Maximum
Long Call	–4.28%	–99.63%	–68.34%	–26.87%	35.62%	701.07%
Short Put	14.50%	–544.27%	–17.12%	32.80%	66.76%	98.39%

Bearish Directional Trades

Bearish directional trades apply to stocks with large negative earnings announcement returns. Results from two bearish trades were compared: long puts versus short calls. Bearish trades were established one day after the earnings announcements and held for 22 trading days. The strike prices were at-the-money or near-the-money, and the expiration dates were at least two months after the position was established. Table 9.5 presents the results for stocks with less than –5% earnings announcement returns.

The results of long puts were studied first. Long puts for negative PEAD were not profitable. On average, long put strategy returns were –14.33%. The median return was worse, at –29.35%. Long puts performed worse than long calls because stocks with large negative earnings announcement returns advanced in the month after the announcements, albeit less than other stocks (see Tables 9.1 and 9.2). Nevertheless, time decay played a big role in the bad performance of long puts.

Even though equity prices moved up for this group, the short call strategy was a big winner. The average return was 9.48%, and the median return was 33.70%. Among the short call trades, 66.04% were positive, compared to 33.40% for long puts.

Table 9.5 Performance of Bearish Directional Trades after Large Negative Earnings Announcement Returns: ±5% Cutoff

CAR ≥ 5%	Mean	Minimum	1st Quartile	Median	3rd Quartile	Maximum
Long Put	−14.33%	−99.35%	−68.13%	−29.35%	19.67%	584.80%
Short Call	9.48%	−610.71%	−25.00%	33.70%	69.72%	98.92%

Table 9.6 repeats the analysis of stocks with less than −8% earnings announcement returns. Both strategies performed better than the 5% cutoff, but the long put strategy was still unprofitable. Once again, the short call strategy was a superior choice over the long put strategy to exploit negative PEAD.

Table 9.6 Performance of Bearish Directional Trades after Large Negative Earnings Announcement Returns: ±8% Cutoff

CAR ≥ 8%	Mean	Minimum	1st Quartile	Median	3rd Quartile	Maximum
Long Put	−12.14%	−99.35%	−65.96%	−26.44%	23.35%	404.40%
Short Call	12.59%	−589.43%	−21.79%	38.11%	70.67%	98.86%

Time Series Analysis

As we have done with prior chapters, we now present the annual analysis of the overall results. Mean returns with the ±5% cutoff are emphasized. Figure 9.1 presents mean returns from two bullish options plays (long calls and short puts) implemented after earnings announcement returns no smaller than 5%. Detailed data are provided in Table A9.1 in the "Appendix" section at the end of this chapter. The short put strategy outperformed the long call strategy in every year. The outperformance was often more than 20% (in seven years), and the largest outperformance was 31% (2001). The long call strategy was positive in seven years with a 50% hit ratio, whereas the short put strategy was positive in 12 years with an 86% hit ratio. The median return (reported in the "Appendix" section) was positive in every year for the short put strategy, and was positive in only one year (1996) for the long call strategy. Even in 1999, when the average returns of the two bullish trades were close, the median return of the short put strategy still outperformed that of the long call strategy by 50%. Our evidence suggests that the short put strategy is strongly preferred to the long call strategy when exploiting positive PEAD, unless the underlying stock is expected to go through a phenomenal uptrend. The results of bullish trades for 8% cutoff are presented in Table A9.2 in the "Appendix" section.

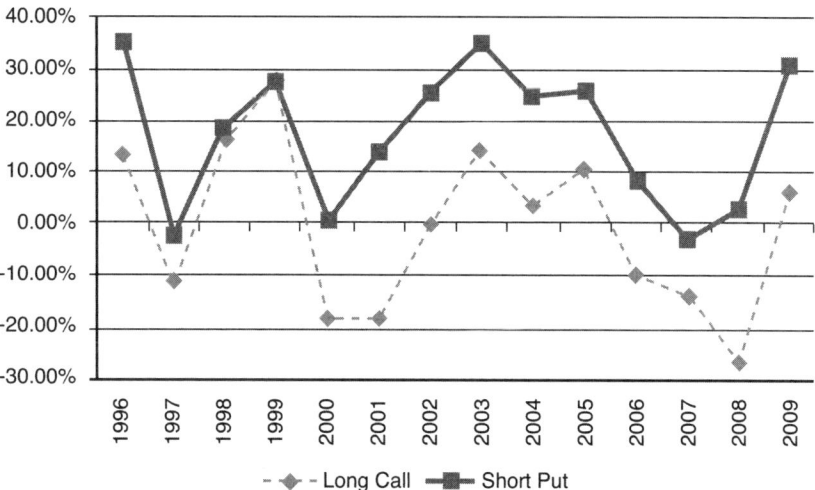

Figure 9.1 Annual performance of long calls and short puts after large positive earnings announcement returns.

Figure 9.2 presents the mean returns of the two bearish trades (long puts and short calls) for each year from 1996 to 2009. Detailed data are also provided in Table A9.3 in the "Appendix" section. The short call strategy outperformed the long put strategy in every year. The outperformance was more than 20% in ten of the years. Whereas the short call strategy was profitable in 11 of the 14 years, the long put strategy was profitable in only 3 years. The median return for the short call strategy was positive every year, whereas the median long put strategy was negative every year. The evidence clearly points to the short call strategy as the preferred choice to exploit negative PEAD. The results of the bearish trades for the 8% cutoff are presented in Table A9.4 in the "Appendix" section. The results are largely the same as those for the ±5% cutoff.

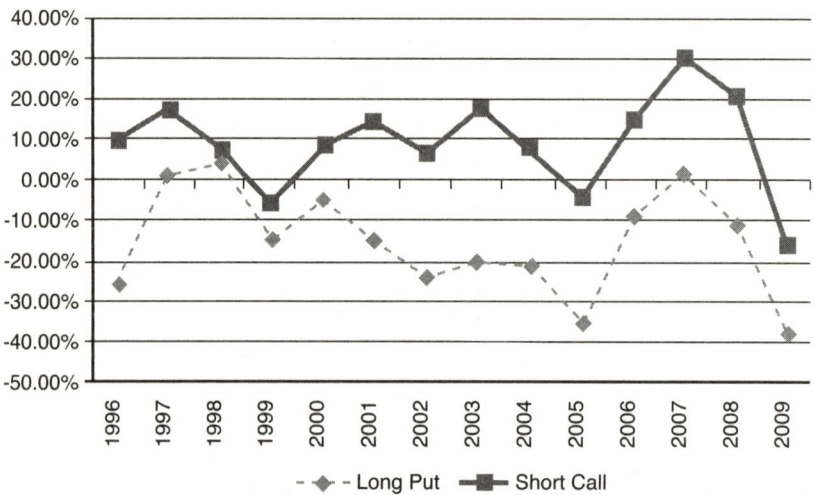

Figure 9.2 Annual performance of long calls and short puts after large negative earnings announcement returns.

The Takeaway

We find a strong post-earnings-announcement drift in our sample. Stocks with large positive earnings announcement returns tend to outperform stocks with large negative earnings announcement returns by a wide margin.

To exploit the drift, we apply bullish directional options trades (long calls and short puts) for stocks with large positive earnings announcement returns and bearish directional trades (long puts and short calls) for stocks with large negative earnings announcement returns. The evidence strongly suggests that investors can profit with options by exploiting post-earnings-announcement drift. However, the choice of option strategies is critical to the success of the trade.

With the help of favorable stock price movements subsequent to earnings announcements and large time decay, shorting puts of stocks experiencing large positive earnings announcement returns is highly profitable. However, long calls of the same stocks were unprofitable because time decay more than offset the positive effect of favorable stock price movement.

Stocks experiencing large negative earnings announcement returns do not decline significantly after earnings announcements. Their prices also advance on average, albeit less so than other stocks. Buying puts of these stocks after earnings announcements was unprofitable due to both large time decay and unfavorable stock price movement. However, shorting calls of such stocks was profitable despite the unfavorable price movement because the positive impact of time decay dominated.

Appendix

Table A9.1 Annual Performance of Bullish Directional Trades after Large Positive Earnings Announcements: ±5% Cutoff

	Long Calls		Short Puts	
Year	*Mean*	*Median*	*Mean*	*Median*
1996	13.74%	5.71%	35.03%	56.86%
1997	−10.82%	−22.40%	−2.25%	23.23%
1998	16.19%	−12.41%	18.75%	38.13%
1999	26.88%	−7.73%	27.11%	42.38%
2000	−17.65%	−44.21%	1.07%	17.50%
2001	−17.77%	−31.82%	14.12%	35.11%
2002	−0.17%	−13.52%	25.20%	37.76%
2003	14.38%	−3.01%	34.72%	50.95%
2004	3.50%	−13.13%	24.89%	43.42%
2005	10.36%	−10.03%	25.56%	42.46%
2006	−10.08%	−24.95%	8.32%	34.03%

	Long Calls		Short Puts	
Year	Mean	Median	Mean	Median
2007	–13.60%	–38.92%	–2.84%	7.11%
2008	–26.02%	–44.07%	2.82%	14.95%
2009	5.82%	–10.64%	30.90%	45.42%

Table A9.2 Annual Performance of Bullish Directional Trades after Large Positive Earnings Announcements: ±8% Cutoff

	Long Calls		Short Puts	
Year	Mean	Median	Mean	Median
1996	9.33%	–0.50%	33.89%	58.52%
1997	–5.28%	–17.22%	3.79%	25.63%
1998	17.06%	–17.69%	21.57%	36.60%
1999	24.59%	–13.66%	23.92%	40.53%
2000	–19.31%	–49.72%	–4.05%	12.31%
2001	–19.03%	–32.60%	10.98%	33.67%
2002	–4.66%	–12.82%	26.19%	36.47%
2003	17.30%	–3.10%	38.13%	50.00%
2004	2.81%	–9.23%	21.68%	34.69%
2005	11.06%	–12.75%	29.99%	41.12%
2006	–7.34%	–21.18%	8.27%	36.27%
2007	–11.69%	–36.08%	–3.11%	10.53%
2008	–33.22%	–49.72%	–0.95%	11.80%
2009	6.33%	–10.00%	30.73%	44.81%

Table A9.3 Annual Performance of Bearish Directional Trades after Large Negative Earnings Announcements: ±5% Cutoff

	Long Calls		Short Puts	
Year	Mean	Median	Mean	Median
1996	–25.42%	–27.87%	9.44%	34.08%
1997	1.06%	–13.68%	17.38%	42.93%
1998	3.93%	–24.65%	7.45%	32.66%
1999	–14.56%	–28.87%	–6.07%	28.93%
2000	–5.26%	–17.33%	9.04%	43.12%

CHAPTER 9 • RIDE THE POST-EARNINGS-ANNOUNCEMENT DRIFT

	Long Calls		Short Puts	
Year	Mean	Median	Mean	Median
2001	–14.75%	–34.09%	14.46%	34.68%
2002	–24.06%	–36.36%	6.47%	30.85%
2003	–20.84%	–27.69%	17.70%	44.44%
2004	–21.36%	–37.17%	7.14%	26.48%
2005	–35.56%	–51.52%	–4.26%	5.04%
2006	–8.38%	–24.62%	15.17%	32.02%
2007	1.42%	–8.70%	30.15%	50.68%
2008	–11.43%	–28.20%	20.80%	39.01%
2009	–37.37%	–56.49%	–15.99%	2.22%

Table A9.4 Annual Performance of Bearish Directional Trades after Large Negative Earnings Announcements: ±8% Cutoff

	Long Calls		Short Puts	
Year	Mean	Median	Mean	Median
1996	–27.39%	–37.75%	9.65%	30.67%
1997	2.89%	–12.36%	15.22%	43.64%
1998	5.49%	–24.47%	8.74%	29.26%
1999	–11.40%	–26.67%	–0.84%	31.10%
2000	–2.98%	–15.51%	14.21%	44.38%
2001	–10.30%	–28.95%	21.35%	40.87%
2002	–16.74%	–30.25%	14.70%	42.91%
2003	–28.66%	–36.33%	11.98%	35.68%
2004	–14.75%	–29.93%	17.65%	37.76%
2005	–39.43%	–52.28%	–1.08%	11.59%
2006	–14.22%	–33.43%	6.84%	21.00%
2007	10.00%	–2.33%	40.37%	58.79%
2008	–11.61%	–27.23%	22.55%	43.56%
2009	–29.85%	–45.07%	–11.80%	17.84%

Part III
Advanced Analysis: Improving the Odds of Winning

We have examined the outcomes of several of the most common option strategies around earnings announcements, including both directional and volatility plays. Our analysis of the data has yielded many interesting and sometimes counter-intuitive findings.

A distinct feature of these analyses is that these strategies were applied to all options meeting the indicated liquidity requirements without consideration for security selection (the only exception was the post-earnings-announcement drift strategy, where predictions of future stock returns were based on earnings announcement returns). In this section, we investigate several signals that are potentially useful to help improve the odds of winning. Because it is extremely difficult to predict the direction of earnings announcement returns, we focus on the volatility trades (straddles and strangles). Option markets offer a rich and rare opportunity to profit from volatility moves without worrying about where the market is headed.

This section is organized as follows. Chapter 10 explores the impact of implied volatility on straddle and strangle strategies. Chapter 11 investigates whether *historical* earnings announcement returns are useful in predicting *future* earnings announcement returns and improving the straddle and strangle strategies' performance. Chapter 12 examines how you should select your securities based on company size. Chapter 13 researches the usefulness of several valuation ratios, signals that are successful in stock selection, in the option markets.

Chapter 14 examines potential industry effects that might lurk in the depths of the data pool. Finally, in Chapter 15, we show how to use these signals to greatly enhance the profits of the volatility strategies around earnings announcements.

10

Implied Volatility

Implied volatility, derived from observed option prices, is arguably the single-most-important variable in option pricing. Both the level and the change of implied volatility are important to option trading around earnings announcements. The level of implied volatility determines the cost of the option, and the change in implied volatility is a major determinant in the change in the option price.

This chapter addresses three issues related to implied volatility. First, we examine the relationships between implied volatility before earnings announcements and the magnitude of earnings announcement returns. If the market is reasonably efficient, we expect to observe that higher implied volatility before earnings announcements are associated with larger absolute earnings announcement returns. Second, we investigate how the performance of long and short straddles/strangles around earnings announcements varies with different levels of implied volatility before announcements. If the options are perfectly priced, the performance of straddles/strangles should be the same regardless of their implied volatility before announcements. It's possible that the options markets aren't perfectly efficient, and some options are priced relatively more expensive than others. The key word here is *relatively* because it is possible that all options will be expensive, but relative expensiveness matters. Third, changes in volatility in both pre- and post-earnings announcements periods are examined. The change in implied volatility (vega) has a direct impact on option prices. In particular, the strategy of buying volatility in periods before earnings announcements is based on the premise that implied volatility will steadily increase in the lead up to the earnings announcement date. Similarly, volatility collapse after earnings announcements is a main source of profits from shorting straddles and strangles around earnings announcements.

Implied Volatility and Absolute Earnings Announcement Returns

Which company do you think is likely to have larger absolute earnings announcement returns, Coca-Cola (NYSE: KO) or Netflix (NASDAQ: NFLX)? If you picked Coca-Cola, maybe you should not be trading. The table below shows the absolute returns of eight quarterly earnings announcements during the most volatile years in the sample (2008 and 2009) for the two companies.

Quarter	Absolute Earnings Announcement Return	
	KO	NFLX
Q1 2008	0.43%	22.20%
Q2 2008	4.41%	7.11%
Q3 2008	4.69%	10.52%
Q4 2008	6.25%	14.39%
Q1 2009	3.16%	6.87%
Q2 2009	3.72%	6.80%
Q3 2009	1.31%	14.71%
Q4 2009	2.17%	26.21%
Average	3.27%	13.60%

The average absolute earnings announcement return for Coca-Cola in these eight quarters was 3.27%, less than a quarter of Netflix's 13.60% average return in the same eight quarters. In fact, the largest absolute earnings announcement return for Coca-Cola (Q4 2008, 6.25%) was smaller than Netflix's smallest return (Q2 2009, 6.80%). Implied volatility on the day before earnings announcements, which is the average of the implied volatility of the near-the-money call and near-the-money put, was much greater for Netflix in every quarter. The average implied volatility for Coca-Cola in the eight quarters was 29.65%; that for Netflix was 73.80%, more than twice as high. So, although Netflix is likely to have larger price reactions to earnings announcements, its options are so expensive that buying straddles or strangles before its earnings announcements is far from a sure bet.

How good is the option market at predicting the magnitude of earnings announcement returns? Let's take a look at the data. Our sample includes only options that meet specific liquidity requirements: (1) the bid-ask spread of the straddle must be no more than 10% of the mid-price, and (2) the bid price of the straddle must be no smaller than $0.60. These two requirements ensure that bid-ask spreads and transaction costs do not take a large toll on profits. The focus was on straddles expiring in the nearest month. The final sample had 16,905 observations.

We first calcuate the mean and median absolute earnings announcement returns based on different levels of implied volatility before earnings announcements. These findings are summarized in Figure 10.1. Detailed data are provided in the "Appendix" section at the end of this chapter (Table A10.1). We classified all options that met liquidity requirements into six implied volatility groups. Rounded cutoff points were applied. The bottom group included all options with implied volatility lower than 30%, and the top group included all options with implied volatility higher than 80%.

The data show that higher implied volatility was associated with larger absolute earnings announcement returns. Mean absolute earnings announcement returns increased from 2.80% for the bottom implied volatility group (implied volatility < 30%) to 10.04% for the top implied volatility group (implied volatility > 80%). Medians exhibited a monotonic pattern just as the means did, although the medians were smaller for all groups, showing that in each implied volatility group there were some outliers.

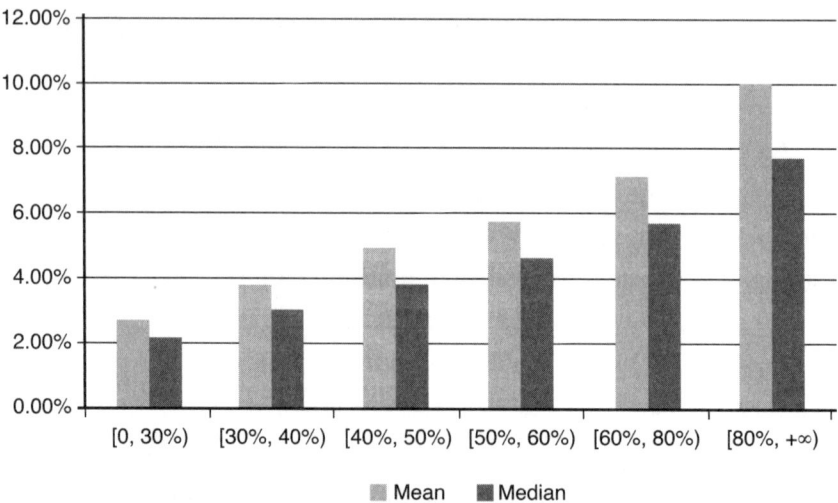

Figure 10.1 Implied volatility and absolute earnings announcement returns.

To learn more about the empirical relation between earnings announcement returns and options implied volatility, we estimated a simple linear regression and generated the following equation:

$$\text{Absolute Earnings Announcement Return} = 0.0091 + 0.0881 \times \text{Implied Volatility} + \varepsilon$$

The regression has a highly significant coefficient on Implied Volatility (with a t-statistic of 59.37) and a respectable adjusted R-square of 17.25%, suggesting that the model fits the data reasonably well and does a decent job of explaining the cross-sectional variation in absolute earnings announcement returns. The positive regression coefficient on Implied Volatility indicates that the higher the implied volatility, the larger the absolute earnings announcement returns. For example, if implied volatility is 50%, the predicted absolute earnings announcement return is 5.32%. If implied volatility increases to 100%, the absolute earnings announcement return is expected to be 9.72%. (This forecast is only an estimate of the *average*.)

Implied Volatility and the Performance of Long and Short Straddles around Earnings Announcements

Our analysis has demonstrated that implied volatility has some predictive power in forecasting the magnitude of future earnings announcement returns. However, we have not addressed the question that is more important to option traders: How does the level of implied volatility affect the performance of the volatility trades around earnings announcements? To answer this question, we compute the performance of long straddles and short straddles conditional on different levels of implied volatility before earnings announcements.

Long straddle results are reported in Table 10.1. The conservative 75% rule (see Chapter 3, "Liquidity Risk: Bid-Ask Spreads") is used for option return calculations. In Chapter 6, "Long Volatility Trades," we found that a long straddle around earnings announcements is generally unprofitable. This is true for all six implied volatility groups because the means are all negative. The medians are all negative as well, indicating that the hit ratios for all six groups are below 50%. The means are less negative than the medians because of the asymmetric returns of long straddles: The downside of the strategy is capped at –100%, but the upside can be much higher than 100%. Minimum and maximum returns confirm the asymmetric return distribution.

Table 10.1 Implied Volatility and the Performance of Long Straddles

Implied Volatility	Obs.	Mean	Minimum	1st Quartile	Median	3rd Quartile	Maximum
[0, 30%)	2529	–1.79%	–68.21%	–18.62%	–9.39%	6.34%	244.85%
[30%, 40%)	3313	–2.80%	–72.31%	–18.89%	–9.52%	5.23%	290.99%
[40%, 50%)	3254	–3.56%	–67.60%	–19.76%	–9.48%	5.02%	253.93%
[50%, 60%)	2374	–4.38%	–70.43%	–19.35%	–9.24%	4.04%	170.04%
[60%, 80%)	2844	–4.66%	–74.80%	–19.38%	–8.46%	4.15%	278.86%
[80%, +∞)	2591	–5.10%	–75.95%	–18.42%	–8.65%	2.76%	252.53%

The most important observation in Table 10.1 is that the return of the long straddles monotonically *decreases* with levels of implied volatility. For the lowest implied volatility group, the mean return of long straddles was −1.79%, whereas the highest implied volatility group was −5.10%, almost three times higher. A closer examination of the return distribution reveals that better performance of options with lower implied volatility comes from a handful of surprising announcements. The 3rd Quartile return for the lowest implied volatility group, 6.34%, was the highest of all groups, whereas that for the highest implied volatility group, 2.76%, was the lowest of all groups. However, this was not true for the median or 1st Quartile returns. Although stocks whose options have higher implied volatility are more likely to experience larger absolute earnings announcement returns, higher implied volatility makes these options so expensive that long straddles are in fact less profitable.

Short straddle results are presented in Table 10.2. The results are the exact opposite of the long straddles. Returns of the short straddles monotonically *increase* rather than *decrease* with the level of implied volatility. For example, when implied volatility was lower than 30%, short straddles had average losses of −6.29%, but the loss was reduced to −1.85% when implied volatility was higher than 80%. The 1st Quartile, median, and 3rd Quartile returns exhibited similar results. The message is clear: Although stocks whose options have higher implied volatility tend to have larger earnings announcement returns, the options are priced so expensively that shorting them was more profitable than buying them.

Table 10.2 Implied Volatility and the Performance of Short Straddles

Implied Volatility	Obs.	Mean	Minimum	1st Quartile	Median	3rd Quartile	Maximum
[0, 30%)	2529	−6.29%	−269.18%	−15.15%	1.62%	11.90%	63.47%
[30%, 40%)	3313	−4.85%	−314.54%	−13.32%	2.05%	12.42%	68.25%
[40%, 50%)	3254	−3.92%	−265.92%	−13.00%	2.49%	13.30%	61.76%
[50%, 60%)	2374	−3.17%	−187.34%	−11.98%	1.91%	12.50%	65.51%

Implied Volatility	Obs.	Mean	Minimum	1st Quartile	Median	3rd Quartile	Maximum
[60%, 80%)	2844	−2.71%	−315.38%	−12.16%	1.60%	12.78%	71.01%
[80%, +∞)	2591	−1.85%	−263.18%	−10.51%	1.95%	12.50%	72.40%

The hit ratios of long and short straddle strategies around earnings announcements for different levels of pre-announcement implied volatility are shown in Figure 10.2. Detailed data behind Figure 10.2 are provided in the "Appendix" section (Table A10.2). Hit ratios were substantially higher for short straddles than for long straddles. Hit ratios for long straddles hovered around 30%, while the hit ratios for short straddles were all over 50%.

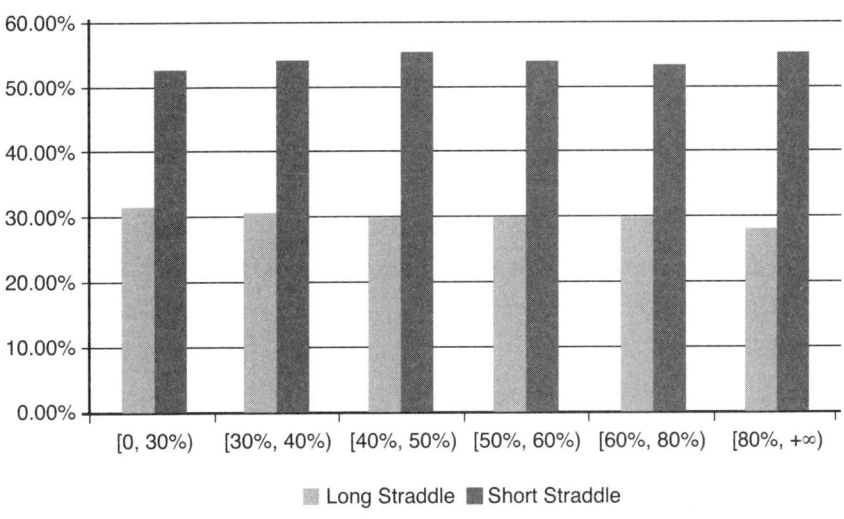

Figure 10.2 Implied volatility and hit ratios of long and short straddles.

The hit ratio for long straddles decreased with the level of implied volatility. For example, the hit ratio was 31.87% for the lowest implied volatility group, and that number dropped to 28.48% for the highest implied volatility group. The hit ratio for short straddles was higher for the high implied volatility options: Hit ratios increased from 53.26% for the lowest implied volatility group to 55.11% for the highest implied volatility group. However, the hit ratio did not increase monotonically with implied volatility. The group with implied volatility between 40% and 50% (the third lowest) had the highest hit ratio of 55.38%.

The results from both longing and shorting straddles shed new light on the conventional wisdom of "buy low, sell high." The existence of low implied volatility reflected the market's consensus that upcoming earnings announcement returns would be muted, which seems to suggest that options of such stocks are poor candidates for long straddles. However, these options were also cheap. If nothing happened, you did not lose much. But if there were any surprises, the payoff would be substantial. Straddle sellers, on the other hand, were better off selling expensive options. The underlying stocks were expected to have large earnings announcement returns, and many of them did. However, the market was anticipating precisely such large movements, so the options were priced very expensively. Shorting such options was like selling catastrophe insurance. The insurance was expensive because the likelihood of a disaster was more than just a remote chance. However, the potential loss for the seller was manageable. If there was no disaster, the seller pocketed a hefty premium.

The Evolution of Implied Volatility around Earnings Announcements

Unlike earnings announcement returns, which are highly unpredictable, the evolution or change of implied volatility around earnings announcements exhibits a strong and repeated pattern. Figure 10.3 depicts average implied volatility in the seven days around earnings announcements (i.e., day t–5 to day t+1) for different implied volatility levels. Detailed data are provided in the "Appendix" section (Table A10.3). The observations are segregated into six portfolios based on implied volatility. The lowest portfolio had implied volatility less than 30% and the highest portfolio had implied volatility higher than 80%. Options were at-the-money or near-the-money with the earliest expiration dates. Implied volatility was measured five days before the earnings announcements (i.e., day t–5). This treatment was necessary to avoid "look-ahead bias."

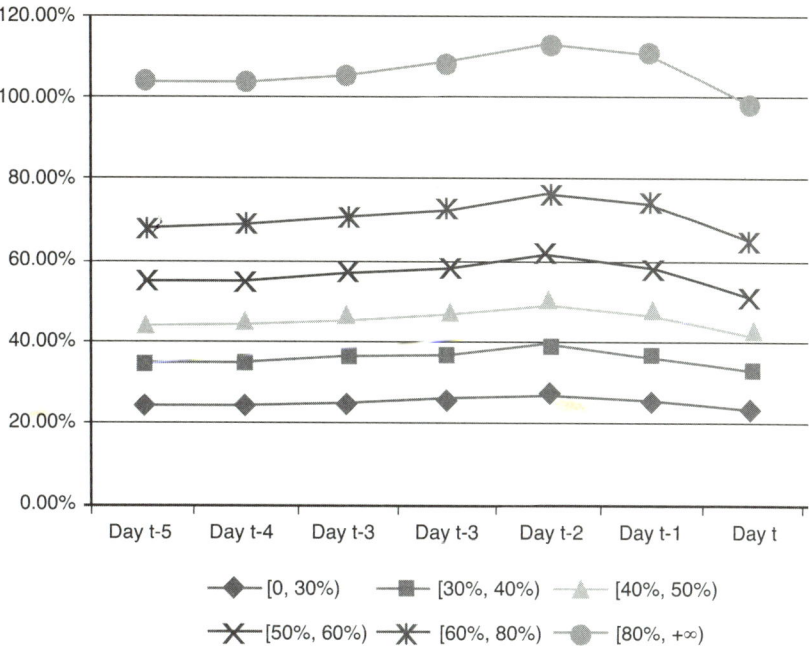

Figure 10.3 Evolution of implied volatility around earnings announcements.

For all groups, implied volatility gradually rose in the days before earnings announcements, reflecting traders' increasing anxiety as earnings announcement dates approached. Implied volatility reached a peak on the day before the announcements. This pattern of increasing volatility leading up to earnings announcements was the basis for the long volatility strategy described in Chapter 8, "Buy Volatility before Earnings Announcements." Despite the popularity of the strategy, our research shows that this strategy is generally unprofitable when applied to a large sample of options.

There were two reasons that the strategy was not nearly as profitable as many traders believe. The first is time decay, which was problematic for long straddles with short duration. Second, as reflected in Figure 10.3, increases in implied volatility are generally not large enough to make the long straddle profitable.

Figure 10.4 shows the mean returns of long/short straddles for six implied volatility groups *before* earnings announcements. Detailed data are provided in the "Appendix" section (Table A10.4). In both strategies, long or short straddles were established five days prior to earnings announcements and closed one day before the announcements.

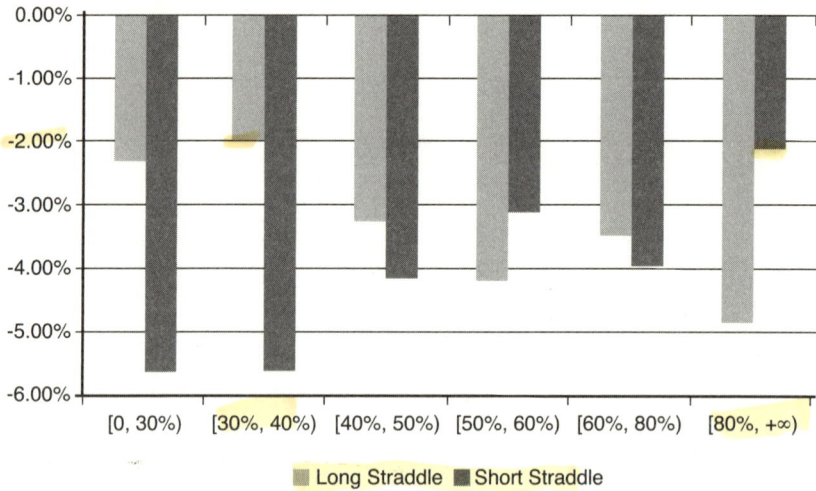

Figure 10.4 Performance of long and short straddles before earnings announcements, conditional on implied volatility five days prior to announcements: day t−5 to day t−1.

The results suggest that straddle buyers are better off with inexpensive straddles (in terms of implied volatility), whereas straddle sellers should sell expensive straddles (in terms of implied volatility). Long straddles in the lowest implied volatility group had average returns of −2.34%, and long straddles in the highest implied volatility group had average returns of −4.85%. For straddle sellers, the opposite is true. Selling straddles in the lowest implied volatility group had average returns of –5.67%, whereas selling straddles in the highest implied volatility reduced losses to –2.09%.

After earnings and related information are released, implied volatility drops sharply, a phenomenon called *volatility collapse*. Figure 10.3 shows this volatility collapse. Within two days, implied volatility for all groups dropped below its seven-day level (i.e., day t–5). Volatility collapse was more salient for higher implied volatility groups because these stocks had more uncertainty coming into earnings announcements (and therefore more uncertainty *resolved* upon the earnings announcement itself). Figure 10.5 reports mean returns of buying and shorting straddles in the two days around earnings announcements. Detailed data are provided in the "Appendix" section (Table A10.5). A straddle is bought or sold the day before earnings announcements and closed two days after the announcements. These trades were similar to those in Tables 10.1 and 10.2. The difference is that in Figure 10.5 implied volatility groups were based on the close six days prior to earnings announcements, whereas in Tables 10.1 and 10.2, groups were formed based on the close one day before earnings announcements.

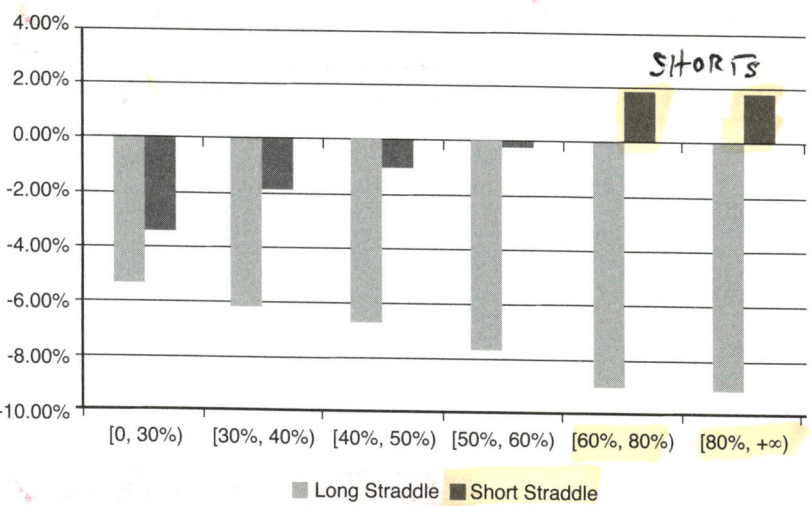

Figure 10.5 Performance of long and short straddles around earnings announcements, conditional on implied volatility five days prior to announcements: day t and day t+1.

Over the two-day holding period, long straddles were inferior to short straddles in all implied volatility groups. This was due to both volatility collapse and time decay favoring short straddles. "Buy-low, sell-high" works: Straddle buyers should aim at inexpensive straddles, and straddle sellers should focus on expensive ones. Long straddles in the lowest implied volatility group had an average return of –5.38%, whereas long straddles in the highest implied volatility had an average return of –9.13%. Short straddles in the lowest implied volatility group had an average return of –3.32%, and short straddles in the highest implied volatility actually turned in gains of 1.82% on average.

The Takeaway

Implied volatility before earnings announcements reflects the market's consensus of uncertainty regarding the information that is about to be released in the imminent announcements. Through both regression and portfolio analyses, we found that the level of implied volatility was an impressive predictor of the magnitude of earnings announcement returns. Very high implied volatility forecasted large price reactions to earnings announcements, and very low implied volatility predicted muted market reactions to earnings news.

However, the positive relationship between implied volatility and absolute future earnings announcement returns does not necessarily imply that volatility buyers should buy options with high implied volatility and volatility sellers should focus on options with low implied volatility. On the contrary, we found that volatility buyers should prefer low implied volatility options to high implied volatility options, even though high implied volatility predicts larger market reactions. For volatility sellers, high implied volatility options were better choices than low volatility options. Implied volatility is typically higher than realized volatility. The gap was even bigger for high implied volatility positions, making them better candidates for shorting. Prices of low implied volatility options, on the other hand, can spike from time to time because expectations are so low.

Implied volatility generally increases before earnings announcements and collapses after earnings announcements. However, rises in implied volatility before the announcements were relatively small. This small rise was insufficient to offset time decay, so buying straddles or strangles before the announcements was on average unprofitable. Volatility collapse after earnings announcements was sharp, especially for high implied volatility options. This fact helps explain why high implied volatility options are good candidates for shorting.

Appendix

Table A10.1 Levels of Implied Volatility and Distribution of Future Absolute Earnings Announcement Returns

Implied Volatility	No. of Obs.	Mean	Minimum	1st Quartile	Median	3rd Quartile	Maximum
[0, 30%)	2529	2.80%	0.00%	1.00%	2.14%	3.90%	24.93%
[30%, 40%)	3313	3.90%	0.00%	1.45%	3.09%	5.39%	23.65%
[40%, 50%)	3254	4.93%	0.00%	1.88%	3.89%	6.82%	33.80%
[50%, 60%)	2374	5.90%	0.00%	2.36%	4.80%	8.24%	31.91%
[60%, 80%)	2844	7.18%	0.00%	2.70%	5.78%	10.21%	43.88%
[80%, +∞)	2591	10.04%	0.00%	3.49%	7.74%	13.92%	63.76%

Table A10.2 Levels of Implied Volatility and Hit Ratios of Long and Short Straddles

Implied Volatility	Long Straddle	Short Straddle
[0, 30%)	31.87%	53.26%
[30%, 40%)	30.94%	54.69%
[40%, 50%)	30.27%	55.38%
[50%, 60%)	30.29%	54.42%
[60%, 80%)	30.45%	53.48%
[80%, +∞)	28.48%	55.11%

Table A10.3 Evolution of Implied Volatility around Earnings Announcements

Implied Volatility	Day t–5	Day t–4	Day t–3	Day t–2	Day t–1	Day t	Day t+1
[0, 30%)	24.35%	24.58%	25.10%	25.79%	27.19%	25.15%	23.68%
[30%, 40%)	35.10%	35.38%	36.24%	37.34%	39.33%	36.78%	33.61%
[40%, 50%)	44.83%	45.23%	46.18%	47.53%	49.95%	47.66%	42.32%
[50%, 60%)	54.65%	55.02%	56.33%	58.03%	61.03%	58.49%	51.29%
[60%, 80%)	68.50%	69.05%	70.33%	72.33%	75.73%	73.74%	64.41%
[80%, +∞)	104.07%	104.28%	105.52%	108.42%	113.28%	110.78%	98.28%

Table A10.4 Performance of Long and Short Straddles before Earnings Announcements, Conditional on Implied Volatility Five Days Prior to Announcements: Day t–5 to Day t–1

Implied Volatility	Long Straddle	Short Straddle
[0, 30%)	–2.34%	–5.67%
[30%, 40%)	–1.99%	–5.64%
[40%, 50%)	–3.25%	–4.20%
[50%, 60%)	–4.24%	–3.13%
[60%, 80%)	–3.49%	–3.93%
[80%, +∞)	–4.85%	–2.09%

Table A10.5 Performance of Long and Short Straddles before Earnings Announcements, Conditional on Implied Volatility Five Days Prior to Announcements: Day t and Day t+1

Implied Volatility	Long Straddle	Short Straddle
[0, 30%)	–5.38%	–3.32%
[30%, 40%)	–6.28%	–1.84%
[40%, 50%)	–6.80%	–1.09%
[50%, 60%)	–7.71%	–0.19%
[60%, 80%)	–9.03%	1.31%
[80%, +∞)	–9.13%	1.82%

11

Historical Earnings Announcement Returns

Mark Twain famously said, "History doesn't repeat itself, but it does rhyme." Is this true when it comes to forecasting earnings announcement returns? This chapter analyzes two topics related to the usefulness of *historical* earnings announcement returns for options trading around earnings announcements. First, are historical earnings announcement returns useful for forecasting *future* earnings announcement returns? Second, can investors use historical earnings announcement returns to enhance long or short straddle returns?

Historical and Future Earnings Announcement Returns

Suppose you wanted to predict Google's (NASDAQ: GOOG) Q4 2011 earnings announcement return (announced in the after hours of January 19, 2012). You looked up Google's earnings announcement returns over the past four quarters and found the following:

Quarter	*Signed* Return	*Absolute* Return
Q4 2010	−3.15%	3.15%
Q1 2011	−7.91%	7.91%
Q2 2011	11.03%	11.03%
Q3 2011	7.87%	7.87%
Average	1.96%	7.49%

How should you use this historical information? Suppose you applied a simple average of the signed return to make the forecast. You would predict that Google has relatively small earnings announcement returns because the average signed return was less than 2%. However, a close examination of the numbers suggests that this conclusion is misleading. Of the four earnings announcement returns, two were very positive (Q2 2011 and Q3 2011) and the other two were very negative (Q4 2010 and Q1 2011). Three of them had absolute returns higher than 7% and the average absolute return was high at 7.49%. This is hardly the magnitude of earnings announcement returns you expect to see from a boring, stable business. Indeed, Google returned –7.41% in its Q4 2011 earnings announcement.

The previous example suggests that with respect to *signed* earnings announcement returns, historical information does not appear to be very helpful in predicting the future. However, historical information is quite powerful for predicting future *absolute* (unsigned) earnings announcement returns. You might not be able to simultaneously predict the direction and magnitude of returns, but predicting *only* the magnitude is much easier. Is this finding particular to Google or applicable to other stocks? If this finding were an empirical regularity, there would also be implications for how to set up straddles or strangles. We examine these issues using simple linear regressions. The sample includes only stocks with options meeting specific liquidity requirements: (1) the bid-ask spread of the straddle is smaller than 10% of the mid-price and (2) the bid price is greater than $0.60.

In the first regression, we regress future *signed* earnings announcement returns against historical *signed* earnings announcement returns (earnings announcement returns are referred to as "EARET" hereafter). Historical signed EARET was measured as an average of the most recent four quarters' signed EARET. Regression results follow:

Future signed EARET = $0.0031 - 0.0169 \times$ historical signed EARET + ε

The message of the model is that historical signed EARET is useless for predicting future signed EARET. The regression coefficient, –0.0169, is statistically insignificant (t-statistic = –1.13) and the R-squared of the model was close to 0 (meaning that historical signed EARET explained none of the variability of future signed EARET). This result should not be surprising because it is difficult to forecast *signed* EARET.

The situation is dramatically different if we are interested in predicting future *absolute* EARET instead. In this regression, future absolute EARET is regressed against historical absolute EARET. Historical absolute EARET is defined as the average of the most recent four quarters' absolute EARETs. The estimated equation is

Future absolute EARET = 0.0307 + 0.4251 × historical absolute EARET + ε

The regression coefficient, 0.4251, is highly significant (with a t-statistic of 39.54) and its R-squared was 8.57%, which is respectable in the world of empirical finance. According to this model, if historical absolute EARET is 10%, future absolute EARET is predicted to be 7.29%. As we will see shortly, this is a fairly accurate estimate. The equation says that historical absolute EARET is positively associated with future absolute EARET: A stock with large (small) absolute EARET in the past is likely to have large (small) absolute EARET in the future.

Figure 11.1 shows the mean and median absolute EARET based on different levels of historical absolute EARET. Detailed data are provided in the "Appendix" section at the end of the chapter (Table A11.1). These observations are divided into six groups. The six portfolios are segregated into easily digestible cut-off points. The first portfolio included all observations with absolute EARET between 0% and 2%; the second portfolio contained all observations with absolute EARET between 2% and 4%, and the sixth portfolio contained all observations with absolute EARET greater than 12%. The number of observations in each portfolio was not the same, with the first two groups accounting for roughly 40% of the observations.[1]

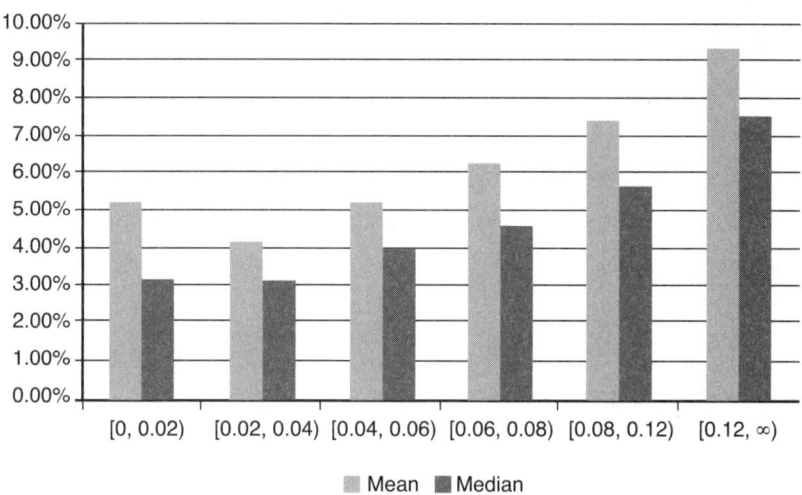

Figure 11.1 Historical absolute EARET and future absolute EARET.

Consistent with the regression analysis, larger historical absolute EARET is associated with larger future absolute EARET. The mean (median) future absolute EARET increased from 5.18% (3.18%) for the bottom group (historical absolute EARET < 0.02) to 9.34% (7.54%) for the top group (historical absolute EARET > 0.12). Volatile businesses (e.g., cyclical industries) are inherently more unpredictable than steady businesses (e.g., utilities). However, there was some convexity in the relation between historical absolute EARET and future absolute EARET. The second group (0.02 ≤ historical absolute EARET < 0.04) had lower absolute future EARET than the bottom group, despite the fact that it had larger absolute EARET in the past. Given that the first two groups account for more than 40%

of the observations, historical absolute EARET is not a very reliable predictor of future absolute EARET return when the return's magnitude is small.

Historical absolute EARET and implied volatility have similar relationships with future absolute EARET. Indeed, Figures 11.1 and 10.1 look alike. When the market sets option prices, historical absolute EARET is an important attribute of the process—the past history of volatility is useful to predict future volatility. Today's implied volatility reflects more timely and relevant information not captured by historical absolute EARET, and that's why implied volatility is a more powerful predictor of future absolute EARET. In fact, the R-squared of the regression doubles when implied volatility replaces historical absolute EARET as the explanatory variable. Should you focus only on implied volatility and get rid of the historical absolute EARET because information in it is possibly subsumed by information in implied volatility? That would be a mistake. Historical absolute EARET and implied volatility contain largely non-overlapping information and one does not subsume the other. A regression of future absolute EARET on both historical absolute EARET and implied volatility follows:

Future Absolute EARET = 0.0061 + 0.1739 × Historical Absolute EARET + 0.0746 × Implied Volatility + ε

Regression coefficients on both historical absolute EARET and implied volatility were statistically significant (t-statistics are 14.71 and 40.73, respectively). Both variables had incremental information about future absolute EARET in the presence of the other variable. You can improve your forecasting accuracy of future absolute EARET by incorporating both pieces of information.

Historical Absolute EARET and the Performance of Long and Short Straddles around Earnings Announcements

The preceding section showed that historical absolute EARET is positively associated with future absolute EARET. Companies with large historical absolute EARET tend to have large future absolute EARET. How relevant is this information to the long/short straddle strategy around earnings announcements? This section addresses this issue.

The performance of the long straddles for each of the six historical absolute EARET portfolios is summarized in Table 11.1. The conservative 75% rule was assumed for return calculations. Average returns for long straddles were negative for all levels of historical absolute EARET. However, unlike the results for implied volatility, stocks with low historical absolute EARET did not have higher average long straddle returns. The range of returns was quite narrow, centering around −3.7%, meaning that the relation between historical absolute EARET and the long straddles' performance is weak.

The median returns were even more negative than the means, because of the right-skewness of the data (that is, the extreme positive returns were much larger, in absolute terms, than the extreme negative returns). The range of returns was tight and there was no clear pattern in the data. The same was observed at other points of the return distribution such as the 1st and 3rd Quartiles.

Table 11.1 Historical Absolute EARET and Performance of Long Straddles

Historical Absolute EARET	Obs.	Mean	Minimum	1st Quartile	Median	3rd Quartile	Maximum
[0, 0.02)	2532	−3.88%	−75.60%	−16.43%	−8.26%	2.84%	210.71%
[0.02, 0.04)	4533	−3.56%	−72.31%	−18.75%	−9.49%	4.51%	278.86%
[0.04, 0.06)	3852	−3.63%	−67.57%	−19.29%	−9.28%	4.87%	290.99%

Historical Absolute EARET	Obs.	Mean	Minimum	1st Quartile	Median	3rd Quartile	Maximum
[0.06, 0.08)	2439	−3.94%	−72.15%	−20.05%	−9.61%	5.13%	235.40%
[0.08, 0.12)	2292	−3.62%	−74.80%	−20.65%	−9.26%	5.51%	252.53%
[0.12, ∞)	1257	−3.48%	−75.95%	−19.91%	−8.14%	5.91%	197.43%

Table 11.2 presents the results for short straddles. As with the long straddles, average returns were negative for all levels of historical absolute EARET. However, the medians were all positive, and the 1st and 3rd Quartile returns were all higher than their counterparts in the long straddles. Median short straddle returns were lowest for the smallest historical absolute EARET group, consistent with the observation that shorting volatility is least profitable for historically stable stocks. Profits from shorting straddles did not increase monotonically with historical absolute EARET, however. The same pattern was observed for other points in the distribution. The relationship between historical absolute EARET and performance of short straddles was not strong.

Table 11.2 Historical Absolute EARET and Performance of Short Straddles

Historical Absolute EARET	Obs.	Mean	Minimum	1st Quartile	Median	3rd Quartile	Maximum
[0, 0.02)	2532	−3.86%	−224.44%	−11.02%	0.65%	9.56%	70.17%
[0.02, 0.04)	4533	−4.04%	−315.38%	−12.40%	2.35%	12.24%	68.25%
[0.04, 0.06)	3852	−3.92%	−314.54%	−13.15%	1.98%	12.72%	65.23%
[0.06, 0.08)	2439	−3.57%	−255.87%	−12.95%	2.52%	13.50%	66.08%
[0.08, 0.12)	2292	−3.69%	−263.18%	−13.86%	2.27%	14.62%	71.01%
[0.12, ∞)	1257	−3.53%	−205.08%	−12.94%	1.71%	13.83%	72.40%

Figure 11.2 shows the hit ratios of long and short straddles for different levels of historical absolute EARET. Detailed data are provided in the "Appendix" section (Table A11.2). Figure 11.2 shows that

the hit ratio was substantially higher for short straddles than for long straddles regardless of levels of historical absolute EARET. Hit ratios were around 30% for long straddles and above 50% for short straddles. However, consistent with the results in Tables 11.1 and 11.2, the hit ratios did not bear a monotonic relation with the level of historical absolute EARET.

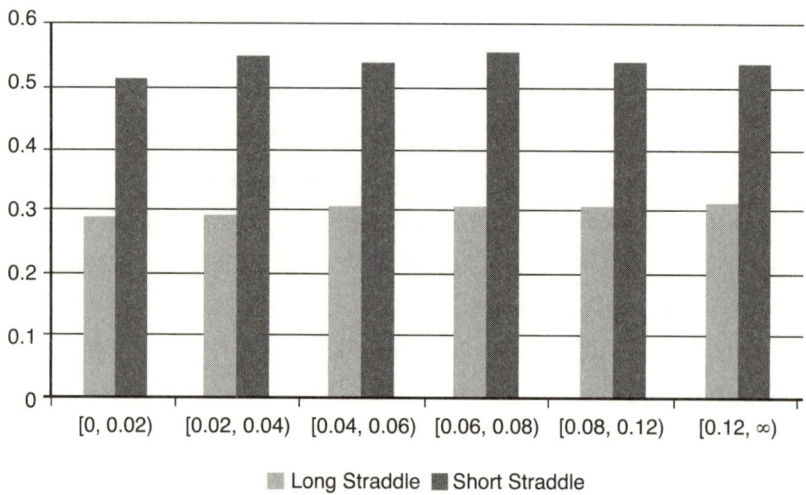

Figure 11.2 Historical absolute EARET and hit ratios of long and short straddles.

The Takeaway

Overall, the results show that history does rhyme, though not perfectly. Historical *signed* EARET is not predictive of future *signed* EARET, but historical *absolute* EARET predicts future *absolute* EARET. Stocks with volatile historical market reactions to earnings announcements tend to have volatile earnings announcement returns in the future. However, the relation between historical and future absolute EARET is not monotonic. Volatile stocks also have higher implied volatility, but the two variables have non-overlapping information when predicting future absolute EARET.

It is slightly better to buy straddles of stocks with larger historical absolute EARET and to sell straddles of stocks with smaller historical absolute EARET. Compared to implied volatility, historical absolute EARET has a much weaker association with the performance of long and short straddles.

Endnote

1. The concentration of stocks in the first two groups is due to the nature of the data (many stocks have relatively uneventful earnings announcements). Dividing the sample into equal-size portfolios has its own problems. For example, if these were evenly divided, the difference in historical absolute EARET between some groups would potentially be too small to make a difference.

Appendix

Table A11.1 Historical Absolute EARET and Future Absolute EARET

Historical Absolute EARET	Obs.	Mean	Minimum	1st Quartile	Median	3rd Quartile	Maximum
[0, 0.02)	2532	5.18%	0.00%	1.35%	3.18%	6.62%	56.12%
[0.02, 0.04)	4533	4.21%	0.00%	1.47%	3.14%	5.58%	48.79%
[0.04, 0.06)	3852	5.30%	0.00%	1.88%	4.02%	7.25%	53.12%
[0.06, 0.08)	2439	6.26%	0.00%	2.23%	4.62%	8.58%	57.55%
[0.08, 0.12)	2292	7.37%	0.00%	2.83%	5.77%	10.18%	56.96%
[0.12, ∞)	1257	9.34%	0.00%	3.37%	7.54%	13.05%	63.76%

Table A11.2 Historical Absolute EARET and Hit Ratios of Long and Short Straddles

Historical Absolute EARET	Long Straddles	Short Straddles
[0, 0.02)	29.11%	51.70%
[0.02, 0.04)	29.76%	55.48%
[0.04, 0.06)	30.87%	54.28%
[0.06, 0.08)	30.91%	55.76%
[0.08, 0.12)	31.11%	54.54%
[0.12, ∞)	31.58%	53.86%

12

Market Capitalization

A stock's market capitalization, or market cap, is the total value of its common equity based on its current market price—the stock price multiplied by the number of common shares outstanding. Although other metrics such as total assets, sales, and earnings are also used to measure a firm's size, market cap is the only market-based metric. (The others are accounting-based.) Stocks are often classified into different groups based on their market cap. There is no definitive rule on how a firm is assigned into a particular market-cap group, however.

In the U.S. stock market, "large cap" stocks typically have more than $10 billion market cap, and "small cap" stocks usually have less than $2 billion market cap. Large-cap stocks are likely to act as leaders and major players in their industries, with higher sales and profits, more employees, and a larger market share than their competitors; and they tend to grow at a slower pace. Small-cap stocks, on the other hand, tend to be younger, nimbler, and full of both potential and risks. Compared to small-cap stocks, large-cap stocks are more closely monitored by investors and regulators due to their influence on the overall economy and the investment dollars they absorb. They also have a large sell-side analyst following, which ensures that there are very knowledgeable information intermediaries that are constantly monitoring and publishing their thoughts and opinions about the companies. This implies that large-cap stocks are less likely to surprise investors during their earnings announcements because much of the information that the company releases during the announcement has already trickled into the marketplace. On the other hand, small-cap stocks are often "off the radar," have a very thin (if any) analyst following, and hence are more likely to surprise investors with the information contained in their earnings announcements.

This chapter provides detailed analysis on the usefulness of a stock's market cap for option trading around earnings announcements. We address two main questions in this chapter: First, does a stock's market cap help forecast future absolute earnings announcement returns? Second, does market cap affect the performance of long and short volatility trades around earnings announcements?

Market Cap and Absolute Earnings Announcement Returns

Exxon Mobil (NYSE: XOM) is the largest integrated oil and gas company and until recently, was the largest company by market capitalization in the U.S. for years. Stone Energy Corp (NYSE: SGY) is also an independent integrated oil and gas company, but much smaller than Exxon Mobil. By the end of 2011, Exxon Mobil had roughly $400 billion market cap, whereas Stone Energy's market cap was about $1.3 billion or about 0.32% of Exxon's. XOM is followed by about 20 analysts, whereas the number of analysts following Stone Energy is about half of that. These two companies operate in the same line of business; and though no two companies are alike, most macroeconomic factors should have a similar impact on each company. The following table lists the absolute returns for the 12 quarterly earnings announcements from 2009 to 2011 for both companies.

Quarter	Absolute Earnings Announcement Returns	
	XOM	SGY
Q1 2009	0.63%	0.76%
Q2 2009	1.46%	26.87%

Quarter	Absolute Earnings Announcement Returns	
Q3 2009	2.94%	17.68%
Q4 2009	3.93%	3.10%
Q1 2010	2.05%	8.55%
Q2 2010	2.02%	14.88%
Q3 2010	1.25%	6.38%
Q4 2010	6.23%	8.42%
Q1 2011	0.23%	7.24%
Q2 2011	4.23%	2.57%
Q3 2011	0.51%	4.36%
Q4 2011	1.78%	0.89%
Average	2.27%	8.48%

From 2009 to 2011, the average absolute quarterly earnings announcement return was 8.48% for Stone Energy, or 3.74 times that of Exxon Mobil (2.27%). The comparison suggests that large-cap stocks tend to have less volatile earnings announcement returns. Is this a general phenomenon? We answer this question by estimating another linear regression. We regress future absolute earnings announcement returns against a rank variable based on market cap.[1] All stocks were ranked based on market cap into quintile portfolios with the smallest stocks in Quintile 1 and the largest stocks in Quintile 5. The sample includes only stocks whose options met specific liquidity requirements: (1) the bid-ask spread of straddles was smaller than 10% of the mid-price, and (2) the bid price of the straddle was greater than $0.60. The estimated equation is as follows:

$$\text{Absolute Earnings Announcement Return} = 0.0741 - 0.0092 \times \text{Market Cap Rank} + \varepsilon$$

The coefficient on market cap rank, −0.0092, was significant (with a t-statistic of −27.40), suggesting that larger stocks tended to have smaller future absolute earnings announcement returns. According to the model, the expected average future absolute earnings announcement return for the smallest stocks was 7.41%, whereas for the largest stocks, it was 3.73%. This result was consistent with the earlier example.

Figure 12.1 shows the mean and median absolute earnings announcement returns for the five market cap quintiles. Detailed data are provided in the "Appendix" section at the end of this chapter (Table A12.1). The graph demonstrates a strong and clear pattern: Both mean and median absolute earnings announcement returns decreased monotonically as market cap increased. The mean (median) absolute earnings announcement return for the smallest stocks (Q1) was 7.89% (6.05%); for the largest stocks (Q5) it was 3.87% (2.89%). These results were close to the regression model's estimates.

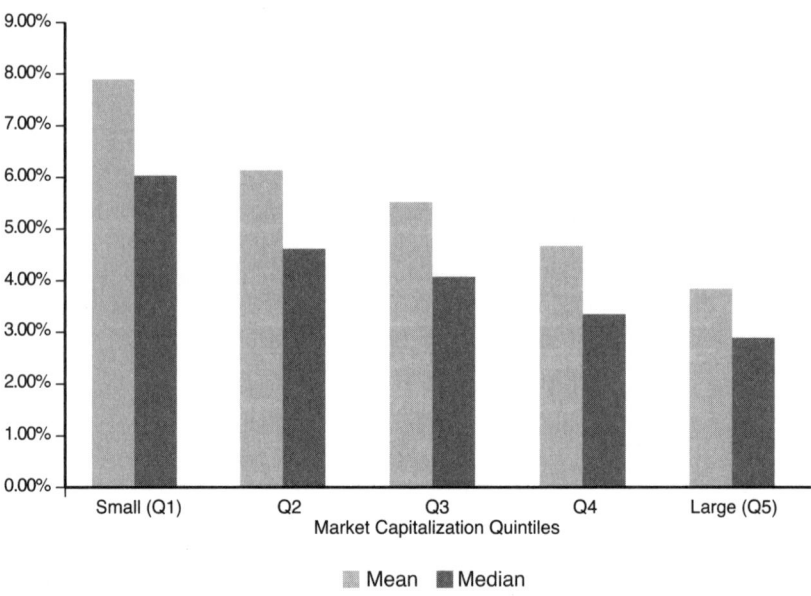

Figure 12.1 Market cap and absolute earnings announcement returns.

Market Cap and Performance of Long and Short Straddles around Earnings Announcements

The preceding section established that market cap is a strong negative predictor of absolute earnings announcement returns. Large-cap stocks tend to have markedly less volatile returns during earnings announcements than small-cap stocks. Does the option market fully price in this information? Does a company's market cap affect the performance of straddles around earnings announcements?

We start by analyzing the impact of market cap on the performance of long straddles. The results are reported in Table 12.1. The conservative 75% rule is applied to option return calculations. Consistent with prior findings, a long straddle is on average unprofitable; the average return of a long straddle is negative for each of the market-cap quintiles. However, the return monotonically decreased with larger market cap. The average return was –2.32% for the smallest stocks and decreased to –4.97% for the largest stocks. The same pattern was observed for the 1st Quartile, median, and 3rd Quartile returns. The results suggest that long straddles are more profitable for small-cap stocks than for large-cap stocks.

Table 12.1 Market Cap and Performance of Long Straddles

Market Cap Quintile	Mean	Minimum	1st Quartile	Median	3rd Quartile	Maximum
Small (Q1)	–2.32%	–67.10%	–18.39%	–8.02%	6.16%	290.99%
Q2	–3.69%	–72.15%	–19.23%	–8.87%	4.38%	235.40%
Q3	–3.59%	–75.60%	–19.91%	–9.74%	5.20%	244.85%
Q4	–4.23%	–74.80%	–20.06%	–10.30%	3.52%	211.83%
Large (Q5)	–4.97%	–75.95%	–20.34%	–10.08%	4.14%	253.93%

Table 12.2 presents results for short straddles. As with the long straddles, average returns of the short straddles were also negative for all market-cap quintiles. However, medians were all positive, and

the 1st and 3rd Quartile returns were all much larger than their counterparts in the long straddle, suggesting that selling volatility around earnings announcements was more profitable than buying volatility. The cross-sectional difference was also interesting. As a mirror image of the long straddle, returns of the short straddle monotonically increased with larger market cap. The mean (median) return of short straddles was −6.30% (0.00%) for small-cap stocks, and −1.31% (3.94%) for large-cap stocks. Thus, it is more profitable to short volatility for large-cap stocks than for small-cap stocks, perhaps because large-cap stocks are less likely to have large surprises.

Table 12.2 Market Cap and Performance of Short Straddles

Market Cap Quintile	Mean	Minimum	1st Quartile	Median	3rd Quartile	Maximum
Small (Q1)	−6.30%	−315.38%	−15.33%	0.00%	10.46%	61.99%
Q2	−4.37%	−255.87%	−13.02%	1.20%	12.04%	67.97%
Q3	−3.87%	−269.18%	−13.02%	2.64%	13.64%	70.17%
Q4	−2.75%	−231.23%	−11.28%	3.50%	14.09%	71.01%
Large (Q5)	−1.31%	−265.92%	−11.22%	3.94%	14.63%	72.40%

Hit ratios for the long and short straddles for market-cap quintiles are summarized in Figure 12.2. Detailed data for the figure are provided in the "Appendix" section (Table A12.2). There are two important observations. First, the hit ratio was substantially higher for short straddles than for long straddles, regardless of the size of the underlying stocks. Second, hit ratios varied with the stocks' market cap: Hit ratios of short straddles increased with the stocks' market cap, whereas hit ratios of long straddles decreased with a stocks' market cap. For example, the hit ratio of the short straddle for the smallest stocks was about 49%, but it was 59% when the strategy was applied to the largest stocks. The cross-sectional variation was considerably smaller for hit ratios of long straddles. Hit ratios of long straddles were about 32% for the smallest stocks, and they dropped merely 2% to 30% when the strategy was applied to the largest stocks.

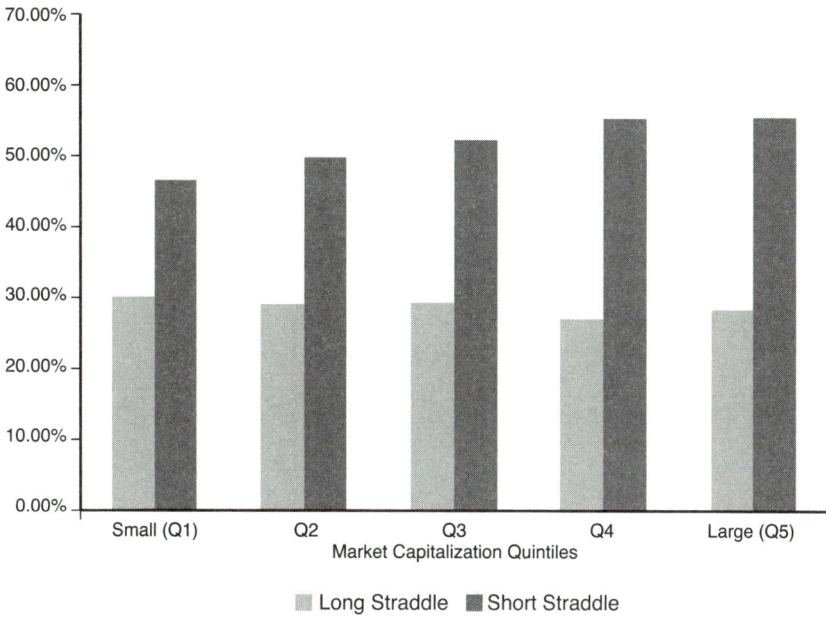

Figure 12.2 Market cap and hit ratios of long and short straddles.

The Takeaway

Compared to small-cap stocks, large-cap stocks are more closely followed and researched by investors and heavily owned by institutional investors. These factors made earnings announcement returns of large-cap stocks much less volatile than those of small-cap stocks.

The negative relation between market cap and future absolute earnings announcement returns is useful for volatility trades around earnings announcements. In particular, we found that long straddles were more profitable for small-cap stocks, whereas short straddles worked better for large-cap stocks.

Endnotes

1. Rank variables were applied instead of market cap itself because a rank variable mitigates the impact of outliers and the result is more relevant.

Appendix

Table A12.1 Market Cap and Absolute Earnings Announcement Returns

Market-Cap Quintile	Mean	Minimum	1st Quartile	Median	3rd Quartile	Maximum
Q1 (Small)	7.89%	0.00%	2.85%	6.05%	10.91%	59.90%
Q2	6.16%	0.00%	1.99%	4.62%	8.45%	56.96%
Q3	5.54%	0.00%	1.94%	4.08%	7.56%	57.55%
Q4	4.69%	0.00%	1.51%	3.37%	6.18%	56.52%
Q5 (Large)	3.87%	0.00%	1.35%	2.89%	5.24%	35.69%

Table A12.2 Market Cap and Hit Ratios of Long and Short Straddles

Market-Cap Quintile	Long Straddle	Short Straddle
Q1 (Small)	31.84%	49.29%
Q2	30.87%	52.67%
Q3	30.97%	55.33%
Q4	28.53%	58.58%
Q5 (Large)	29.90%	58.73%

13

Valuation

Two companies with similar fundamental measures such as book value, earnings, and sales are often valued differently by the market. One reason for different valuations is the differences in each company's growth potential. For example, if two stocks report the same current earnings per share but one is expected to grow twice as fast as the other, it makes sense for the faster-growing stock to trade at a higher valuation. Another reason is sentiment. If investors' sentiment toward a stock or a sector is high (low), this stock or sector tends to be valued higher (lower) than other stocks or sectors. An example of this explanation is the sky-high valuation of technology stocks during the Internet bubble. Investors were (wrongly) convinced that information technology would lead to a new economy, so they valued technology stocks far beyond reasonable estimates. Yet another reason for different valuations is risk. Discounted cash-flow models suggest that stocks with higher perceived risk will receive lower valuations.

There are good reasons to believe that a stock's valuation could affect the magnitude of its earnings announcement returns. Low-valued stocks tend to have lower growth potential and be more stable and investors are generally not too enthusiastic about these stocks (i.e., investors' sentiment is low). These factors suggest that the absolute earnings announcement returns for low-valued stocks should be smaller than those for high-valued stocks. This is because a stable business is less likely to generate surprises, and any low sentiment that the stock exhibits means that bad news is sort of expected and good news is taken with a grain of salt. The opposite is expected for high-valued stocks. Investors cheer for evidence of continued high growth, sending prices sharply higher; but they can be disappointed by any sign of slower growth, triggering a deep sell-off. The impact of the risk factor on absolute earnings announcement returns is likely to be neutral. Information released during earnings announcements will lead investors to adjust their perception of risk, but it is unclear why and how the adjustment varies with valuation levels.

In this chapter, we analyze the usefulness of valuation ratios on predicting absolute earnings announcement returns and the performance of long and short straddles around earnings announcements. A stock's valuation is usually measured as the ratio of its share price to a fundamental value. We selected three commonly used fundamental metrics: book value, earnings, and sales. Book value is the accounting value of a company's common equity, the sum of initial investment, cumulative retained earnings, and net equity financing (i.e., additional equity offerings less dividends and share repurchases). Earnings are a company's operating results (revenue minus costs/expenses) over a fiscal year. Sales are revenues generated over a year.

Of the three items, book value is the least volatile because it is cumulative in nature so one period's operating performance has a relatively minor impact on it. Earnings are the most volatile item because a company's performance over a year can be greatly influenced by factors outside of management's control, such as economic cycles.

From these three measures, we created three valuation ratios. First, the price-to-book ratio (P/B) is the company's stock price divided by its book value per share. Second, the price-to-earnings ratio (P/E) is the company's stock price divided by its earnings per share. Third, the price-to-sales ratio (P/S) is the company's stock price divided by sales per share. The ratios can be viewed as the market's answer to the question: How much would you pay for one unit of book value (earnings, sales)? The answer is the P/B (P/E, P/S) ratio. Higher values of P/B, P/E, or P/S mean the market assigns a higher valuation to the stock based on book value, earnings or sales, respectively.

Valuation and Absolute Earnings Announcement Returns

Do the valuation ratios help predict absolute earnings announcement returns? We start by examining the price-to-book (P/B) ratio. Our sample includes only those stocks whose options meet specific liquidity requirements: (1) the bid-ask spread of straddles was smaller than 10% of the mid-price of the straddle and (2) the bid price of the straddle was greater than $0.60. We estimate a linear regression by regressing absolute earnings announcement returns against a rank variable based on the most recent end-of-month P/B ratio. All stocks were ranked into quintile portfolios based on their P/B ratios at the most recent month-end before earnings announcements. Stocks with the lowest P/B ratios (Q1, low price per unit of book value) were coded 0; those with the highest P/B ratios (Q5, high price per unit of book value) were coded 4. The estimated regression was as follows:

Absolute Earnings Announcement Return = $0.0498 + 0.0032 \times$ P/B Rank $+ \varepsilon$

The R-squared of the regression was low (0.68%), but the coefficient on P/B rank, 0.0032, was statistically significant (with a t-statistic of 9.63), suggesting that stocks with a higher valuation tended to have larger absolute earnings announcement returns. According to the model, the expected average future absolute earnings announcement return for stocks with the lowest valuation (coded 0) was 4.98%, whereas for stocks with the highest valuation (coded 4), it was 6.26%.

Figure 13.1 shows mean and median absolute earnings announcement returns for the five P/B quintiles. Detailed data are provided in Table A13.1 in the "Appendix" section at the end of this chapter. The graph shows that the first four P/B quintiles had similar absolute earnings announcement returns, but the highest P/B quintile (i.e., the stocks with the highest valuation per unit of book value) had markedly larger absolute earnings announcement returns.

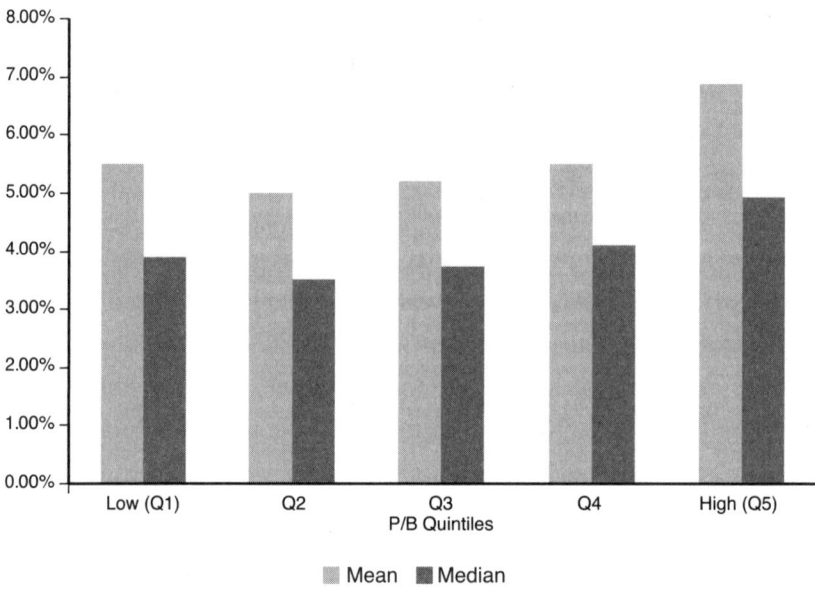

Figure 13.1 P/B and absolute earnings announcement returns.

Next we examine whether price-to-earnings (P/E) ratios have a similar predictability of absolute earnings announcement returns as P/B ratios. We again estimate a linear regression by regressing absolute earnings announcement returns against a rank variable based on the most recent end-of-month P/E ratio. The stocks with the lowest P/E ratios (Q1, low price per unit of earnings) were coded 0, and those with the highest P/E ratios (Q5, high price per unit of earnings) were coded 4. The estimated regression was as follows:

Absolute Earnings Announcement Return = $0.0542 + 0.0010 \times$ P/E Rank $+ \varepsilon$

The R-squared of the regression was very low (0.07%), suggesting the model fit the data poorly. The coefficient on P/E rank, 0.0010, was small but statistically significant (with a t-statistic of 3.04), suggesting a weak positive association between P/E rank and absolute earnings announcement returns.

Figure 13.2 shows mean and median absolute earnings announcement returns for the five P/E quintiles. The detailed data are provided in Table A13.2 in the "Appendix" section. The graph shows a convex U-shaped relationship between P/E ranks and absolute earnings announcement returns. Both low and high P/E stocks had higher absolute earnings announcement returns than stocks with medium P/E ratios. Nevertheless, high P/E stocks (Q5) had the highest mean and median absolute earnings announcement returns. Overall, the results indicated that P/E ratios were less powerful in forecasting absolute earnings announcement returns than P/B ratios, perhaps because P/E ratios are more volatile due to temporary factors that can embed themselves into any given year's earnings.

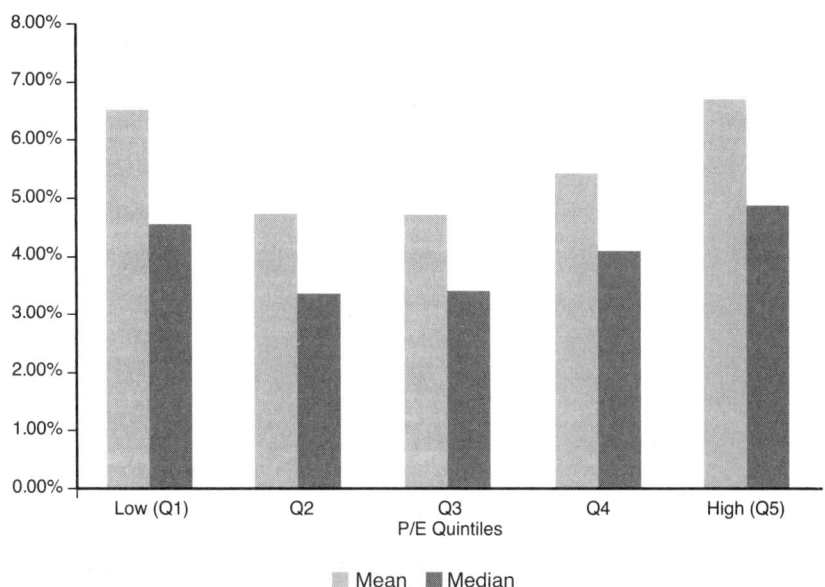

Figure 13.2 P/E and absolute earnings announcement returns.

Lastly, we test whether price-to-sales (P/S) ratios predict absolute earnings announcement returns. We regress absolute earnings announcement returns against a rank variable based on the most recent end-of-month P/S ratio. Stocks with the lowest P/S ratios (Q1, low price per unit of sales) were coded 0, and those with the highest P/S ratios (Q5, high price per unit of sales) were coded 4. The estimated regression was as follows:

Absolute Earnings Announcement Return = $0.0475 + 0.0044 \times$ P/S Rank $+ \varepsilon$

The R-squared of the regression, 1.22%, was low but higher than that of the other two regressions. The coefficient on P/S rank, 0.0044, was larger than the coefficients on P/B rank and P/E rank and statistically significant (with a t-statistic of 12.85), suggesting a strong positive association between P/S rank and absolute earnings announcement returns.

Figure 13.3 shows mean and median absolute earnings announcement returns for the five P/S quintiles. Detailed data are provided in Table A13.3 in the "Appendix" section. This graph is similar to Figure 11.1, but the spread between Q5 and Q1 was much larger, suggesting that P/S ratios were a better predictor of future absolute earnings announcement returns than P/B and P/E ratios. For example, the mean absolute earnings announcement returns for Q1 of P/B, P/E, and P/S were 5.51%, 6.41%, and 5.41%, respectively, whereas those for Q5 of P/B, P/E, and P/S were 6.90%, 6.71%, and 7.11%.

Valuation and Performance of Long Straddles around Earnings Announcements

The preceding section shows that highly valued stocks are more likely to have larger absolute earnings announcement returns. Does the option market take this phenomenon into account? Specifically, we are interested in the cross-sectional variation of the performance of long/short straddles around earnings announcements depending on the valuation ratios.

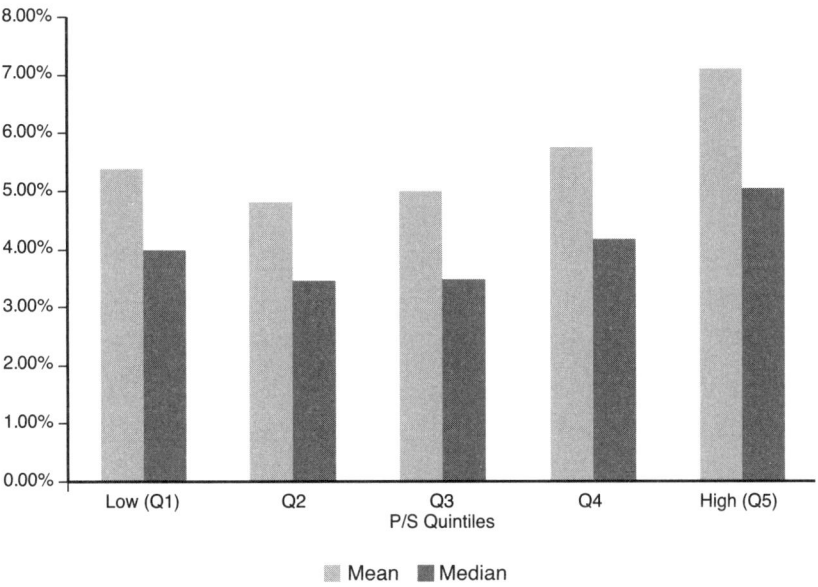

Figure 13.3 P/S and absolute earnings announcement returns.

We start by analyzing the impact of P/B ratios on the performance of long straddles. The results are reported in Table 13.1. The conservative 75% rule was assumed for option return calculations. Performance of long straddles was better for the high P/B stocks (those with high valuation) than for low P/B stocks (those with low valuation). For example, mean (median) returns of long straddles for high P/B stocks (Q5) was –1.34% (–7.30%), whereas that for low P/B stocks (Q1) was –5.44% (–9.96%). The same pattern was observed for 1st and 3rd Quartile returns. In the preceding section we found that high P/B stocks tend to have higher absolute earnings announcement returns than low P/B stocks. This finding might help explain the result in Table 13.1 that long straddles are likely to have better performance with high P/B stocks than with low P/B stocks.

Table 13.1 P/B and Performance of Long Straddles

P/B Quintile	Mean	Minimum	1st Quartile	Median	3rd Quartile	Maximum
Low (Q1)	−5.44%	−69.90%	−19.71%	−9.96%	2.76%	170.04%
Q2	−4.77%	−67.60%	−20.68%	−10.62%	3.38%	253.93%
Q3	−3.86%	−75.60%	−20.16%	−9.85%	4.66%	278.86%
Q4	−3.41%	−72.31%	−19.93%	−9.08%	5.49%	235.40%
High (Q5)	−1.34%	−75.95%	−17.34%	−7.30%	6.60%	290.99%

To examine whether the results in Table 13.1 are sensitive to valuation ratios, we also tested the impact of P/E and P/S ratios on the performance of long straddles. Table 13.2 presents the performance of long straddles around earnings announcements for different P/E ratios. The results for P/E ratios were similar to the results for P/B ratios; the performance of long straddles was much better for high-valuation stocks (those with high P/B or high P/E) than for low-valuation stocks (those with low P/B or low P/E).

Table 13.2 P/E and Performance of Long Straddles

P/E Quintile	Mean	Minimum	1st Quartile	Median	3rd Quartile	Maximum
Low (Q1)	−5.30%	−65.48%	−18.45%	−9.22%	2.19%	244.85%
Q2	−4.92%	−75.60%	−20.42%	−10.27%	4.22%	202.03%
Q3	−3.74%	−71.75%	−21.20%	−10.40%	5.93%	290.99%
Q4	−3.19%	−72.15%	−20.74%	−9.60%	6.40%	235.40%
High (Q5)	−1.64%	−75.95%	−17.17%	−7.62%	5.62%	253.93%

Table 13.3 shows the performance of long straddles around earnings announcements for different P/S ratios. Again, long straddles had better results for high-valued stocks (those with high P/S) than for low-valued stocks (those with low P/S). The consistent results in Tables 13.1, 13.2, and 13.3 reveal that the choice of valuation ratios does not affect the finding that high-valuation stocks are better candidates for long straddles than low-valuation stocks.

Table 13.3 P/S and Performance of Long Straddles

P/E Quintile	Mean	Minimum	1st Quartile	Median	3rd Quartile	Maximum
Low (Q1)	–4.61%	–69.90%	–20.12%	–10.56%	3.79%	244.85%
Q2	–3.89%	–72.31%	–20.33%	–9.80%	5.22%	235.40%
Q3	–3.81%	–75.60%	–19.94%	–9.70%	4.45%	290.99%
Q4	–3.52%	–72.15%	–20.00%	–9.17%	6.13%	191.48%
High (Q5)	–2.98%	–75.95%	–17.37%	–7.85%	4.15%	253.93%

Valuation and Performance of Short Straddles around Earnings Announcements

We now turn to the impact of valuation ratios on the performance of short straddles around earnings announcements. We begin the analysis with the P/B ratio. The results are presented in Table 13.4. In contrast to the results of long straddles, the return of short straddles was higher for low P/B stocks. Mean (median) returns of short straddles for low P/B stocks (Q1) was –2.35% (2.50%), whereas that for high P/B stocks (Q5) was –5.67% (0.60%). The results suggest that investors who want to be short straddles are better off focusing on low P/B stocks rather than high P/B stocks.

Table 13.4 P/B and Performance of Short Straddles

P/E Quintile	Mean	Minimum	1st Quartile	Median	3rd Quartile	Maximum
Low (Q1)	–2.35%	–195.20%	–11.29%	2.50%	13.02%	65.43%
Q2	–2.91%	–269.18%	–11.86%	3.41%	14.19%	65.04%
Q3	–3.76%	–315.38%	–13.02%	2.51%	13.74%	70.17%
Q4	–3.90%	–255.87%	–13.39%	1.95%	13.54%	68.25%
High (Q5)	–5.67%	–314.54%	–14.07%	0.60%	11.36%	72.40%

To examine whether the results in Table 13.4 are sensitive to the choice of valuation ratios, we repeat the analysis with P/E and P/S ratios. Table 13.5 shows how the performance of the short straddles varies with levels of the P/E ratio. The results are similar to those in Table 13.4. Stocks with low P/E ratios were better candidates for short selling of straddles than high P/E stocks.

Table 13.5 P/E and Performance of Short Straddles

P/E Quintile	Mean	Minimum	1st Quartile	Median	3rd Quartile	Maximum
Low (Q1)	–2.07%	–269.18%	–10.39%	2.04%	12.22%	56.02%
Q2	–2.48%	–213.39%	–12.10%	3.35%	14.20%	70.17%
Q3	–4.03%	–315.38%	–14.10%	2.88%	14.37%	67.97%
Q4	–4.49%	–255.87%	–14.73%	2.16%	14.04%	66.08%
High (Q5)	–5.54%	–265.92%	–13.25%	0.82%	10.88%	72.40%

Table 13.6 shows the performance of short straddles for different P/S quintiles. The results are consistent with the results in Table 13.4, suggesting that shorting straddles of low-valuation stocks was more profitable than shorting straddles of high-valuation stocks.

Table 13.6 P/S and Performance of Short Straddles

P/E Quintile	Mean	Minimum	1st Quartile	Median	3rd Quartile	Maximum
Low (Q1)	–3.11%	–269.18%	–12.00%	2.98%	13.83%	65.43%
Q2	–3.80%	–255.87%	–13.79%	2.45%	13.99%	68.25%
Q3	–3.82%	–315.38%	–12.70%	2.37%	13.29%	71.01%
Q4	–3.96%	–210.80%	–14.11%	1.78%	13.14%	67.97%
High (Q5)	–3.89%	–265.92%	–11.72%	1.32%	11.76%	72.40%

Valuation and Hit Ratios of Long and Short Straddles

Hit ratios of long and short straddles for P/B quintiles are presented in Figure 13.4. Detailed data are provided in Table A13.4 in the "Appendix" section. Two notable observations emerge from Figure 13.4. First, the hit ratios are substantially higher for the short straddles than for the long straddles, regardless of valuation levels. The average hit ratio was about 30% for the long straddle strategy, and 55% for the short straddle. Second, hit ratios of long straddles increased monotonically with the P/B ratio, whereas hit ratios of short straddles decreased with the P/B ratio but not monotonically. For long (short) straddles, hit ratios were 6% (4%) higher (lower) for the high P/B stocks (Q5) than for the low P/B stocks (Q1). Figures 13.5 and 13.6 show similar results for the P/E and P/S ratios. Detailed data are provided in Table A13.5 and Table A13.6 in the "Appendix" section, respectively.

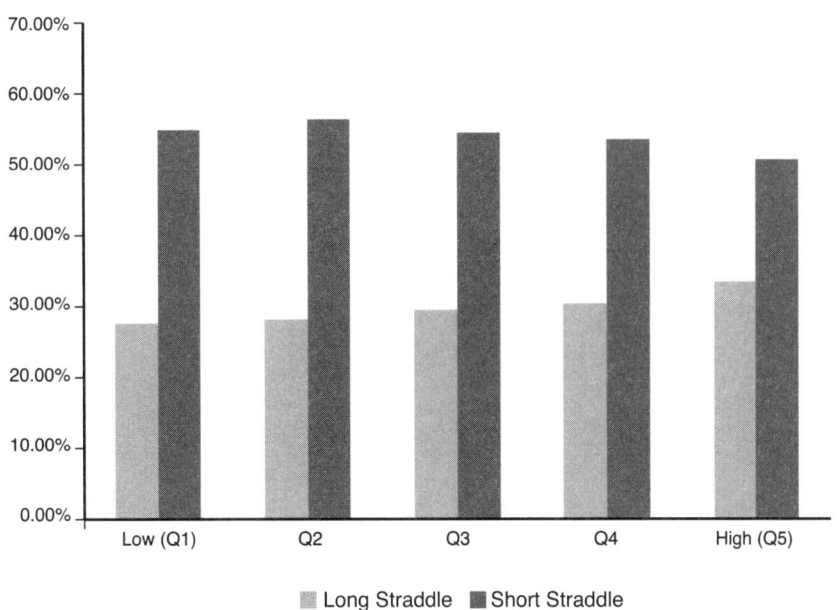

Figure 13.4 P/B and hit ratios of long and short straddles.

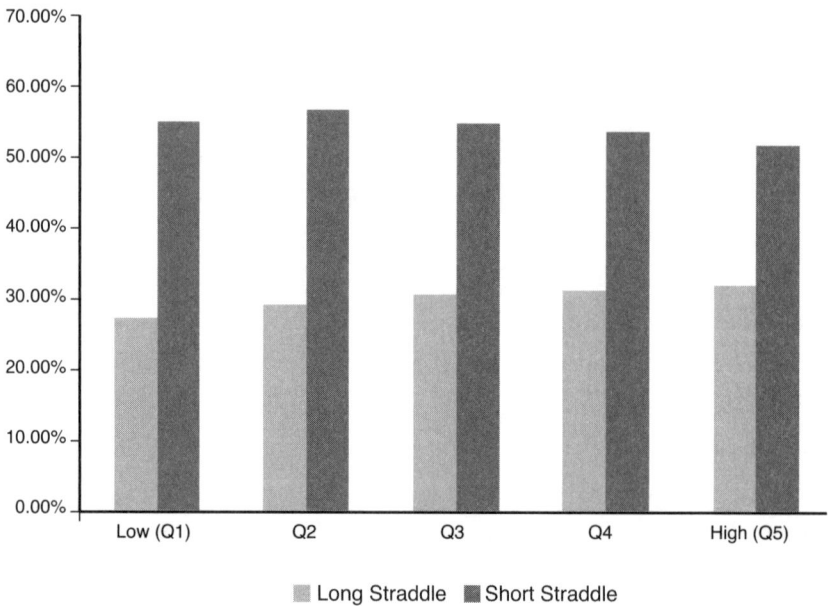

Figure 13.5 P/E and hit ratios of long and short straddles.

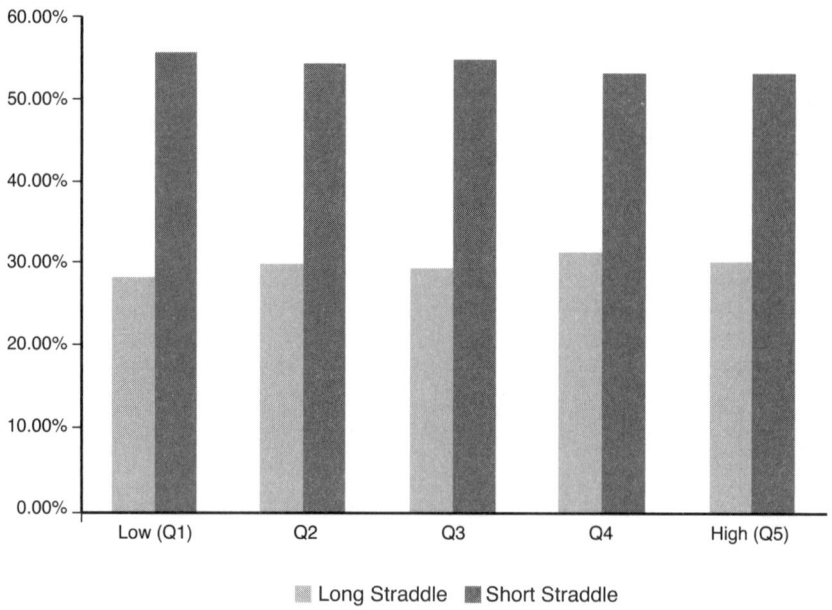

Figure 13.6 P/S and hit ratios of long and short straddles.

The Takeaway

The magnitude of earnings announcement returns is affected by stocks' valuation. Using price-to-book (P/B), price-to-earnings (P/E), and price-to-sales (P/S) ratios to measure stock valuation, we found that stocks with low valuation ratios tended to have less volatile earnings announcement returns, but the relation between valuation ratios and absolute earnings announcement returns was weak.

The performance of long and short straddles can be improved by considering the stock's valuation. In particular, stocks with high valuation ratios were better candidates for straddle buyers, and straddle sellers could make more profits by focusing on stocks with low valuation ratios.

Appendix

Table A13.1 P/B and Absolute Earnings Announcement Returns

P/B Quintile	Mean	Minimum	1st Quartile	Median	3rd Quartile	Maximum
Q1 (Small)	5.51%	0.00%	1.78%	3.91%	7.44%	53.04%
Q2	5.01%	0.00%	1.64%	3.52%	6.69%	55.89%
Q3	5.23%	0.00%	1.69%	3.75%	7.02%	58.58%
Q4	5.51%	0.00%	1.85%	4.12%	7.70%	50.60%
Q5 (Large)	6.90%	0.00%	2.24%	4.94%	9.42%	59.90%

Table A13.2 P/E and Absolute Earnings Announcement Returns

P/E Quintile	Mean	Minimum	1st Quartile	Median	3rd Quartile	Maximum
Q1 (Small)	6.54%	0.00%	2.06%	4.56%	8.77%	59.90%
Q2	4.74%	0.00%	1.58%	3.37%	6.41%	42.91%
Q3	4.72%	0.00%	1.55%	3.40%	6.35%	58.58%
Q4	5.43%	0.00%	1.88%	4.10%	7.67%	35.80%
Q5 (Large)	6.71%	0.00%	2.22%	4.88%	9.13%	57.55%

Table A13.3 P/S and Absolute Earnings Announcement Returns

P/S Quintile	Mean	Minimum	1st Quartile	Median	3rd Quartile	Maximum
Q1 (Small)	5.41%	0.00%	1.85%	4.01%	7.50%	53.04%
Q2	4.82%	0.00%	1.58%	3.46%	6.58%	32.51%
Q3	5.01%	0.00%	1.54%	3.49%	6.69%	42.91%
Q4	5.77%	0.00%	1.92%	4.18%	7.99%	58.58%
Q5 (Large)	7.11%	0.00%	2.36%	5.07%	9.48%	59.90%

Table A13.4 P/B and Hit Ratios of Long and Short Straddles

P/B Quintile	Long Straddle	Short Straddle
Q1 (Small)	28.16%	55.80%
Q2	28.79%	57.33%
Q3	30.09%	55.41%
Q4	30.95%	54.46%
Q5 (Large)	34.11%	51.60%

Table A13.5 P/E and Hit Ratios of Long and Short Straddles

P/E Quintile	Long Straddle	Short Straddle
Q1 (Small)	27.52%	55.56%
Q2	29.56%	57.23%
Q3	31.02%	55.37%
Q4	31.61%	54.15%
Q5 (Large)	32.43%	52.25%

Table A13.6 P/S and Hit Ratios of Long and Short Straddles

P/S Quintile	Long Straddle	Short Straddle
Q1 (Small)	28.93%	56.37%
Q2	30.48%	55.01%
Q3	29.97%	55.44%
Q4	31.97%	53.85%
Q5 (Large)	30.83%	53.87%

14

Industry Effects

The industry in which a company operates is a major determinant of its financial and market performance. Companies in different industries face different levels of competition, regulation, growth opportunities, and other uncertainties. As a result, the predictability of earnings and therefore the volatility of earnings announcement returns can vary greatly across different industries. For instance, all industries can be classified as either pro-cyclical or noncyclical based on their sensitivity to the health of the overall economy. The businesses of pro-cyclical industries, such as automobile manufacturers and airlines, are heavily influenced by business cycles. On the other hand, the noncyclical industries, such as supermarkets and hospitals, provide essential goods and services whose demand is largely unaffected by conditions of the economy. Because business cycles are difficult to predict, earnings and stock returns of pro-cyclical industries exhibit much higher volatility than those of noncyclical industries. The predictability of earnings also varies with industries due to specific risks inherent in each industry. For example, the earnings of companies in the biotechnology industry are less predictable than those in the utilities industry. Advances in science and technology are inherently unpredictable, whereas the prices of electricity, water, and gas are regulated and thus much more stable and predictable.

This chapter analyzes the potential effect of industry membership on the long and short straddle strategy around earnings announcements. We begin by asking whether there are systematic differences in the volatility of earnings announcement returns across industries. Next, we examine how the performance of long and short straddle strategies varies across these different industries.

Industry Classifications

The industry classification system used in this chapter is the GICS (Global Industry Classification Standard), developed by MSCI and Standard and Poor's. This industry classification system was chosen over other systems because it is the industry standard in the global financial community.[1] GICS has four levels of categorization. The first and broadest category is ten sectors. Next are three further, more granular categorizations: 24 industry groups, 68 industries, and 154 sub-industries. Detailed information about the GICS system is found on MSCI's website at www.msci.com.

The analysis in this chapter focuses on the sector level because more granular classifications make results more difficult to track. The ten sectors, which are coded in two-digit numbers, are Energy (10), Materials (15), Industrials (20), Consumer Discretionary (25), Consumer Staples (30), Healthcare (35), Financials (40), Information Technology (45), Telecom Services (50), and Utilities (55). Because the Telecom Services sector has only a handful of stocks, we merged it with the Information Technology sector. Thus, only nine sector results are presented.

Absolute Earnings Announcement Returns by Sector

By the end of 2011, the largest company by market capitalization in the Information Technology sector was Apple (NASDAQ: AAPL), and the largest company by market capitalization in the Utilities sector was Southern Co. (NYSE: SO). The following table lists absolute earnings announcement returns for the two companies for the 12 quarters ending in the fourth quarter of 2011.

Quarter	Absolute Earnings Announcement Returns	
	AAPL	SO
Q1 2009	13.00%	2.37%
Q2 2009	3.00%	0.90%
Q3 2009	2.51%	1.54%
Q4 2009	5.70%	1.77%
Q1 2010	4.14%	1.73%
Q2 2010	4.92%	2.14%
Q3 2010	3.53%	0.04%
Q4 2010	1.67%	0.78%
Q1 2011	2.77%	1.82%
Q2 2011	3.80%	0.07%
Q3 2011	3.51%	1.21%
Q4 2011	5.09%	0.94%
Average	4.47%	1.28%

The average absolute earnings announcement returns over the 12 quarters were 4.47% for Apple but only 1.28% for Southern Co. There was not a single quarter in which Southern Co.'s absolute earnings announcement return was larger than Apple's. This result is well expected, of course, because a technology company such as Apple operates with much more uncertainty than a utility company such as Southern Co. Technological advancement, changes in consumers' preferences, and competition from other corporations such as Samsung and HTC make AAPL's earnings difficult to predict. On the other hand, a regulated utility company's earnings are highly predictable, so the market is less likely to be surprised.

Figure 14.1 shows mean and median absolute earnings announcement returns for the nine sectors. Detailed data are provided in Table

A14.1 in the "Appendix" section at the end of this chapter. This sample includes only stocks whose options before earnings announcements meet specific liquidity requirements. The information technology sector had the highest absolute earnings announcement returns, whereas the utilities sector had the lowest. Mean (median) absolute earnings announcement returns for the information technology sector were 7.80% (5.83%), whereas mean (median) returns for the utilities sector were 2.91% (2.09%), less than half of the information technology sector. In general, cyclical sectors such as energy, materials, industrials, consumer discretionary, and financials tend to have higher absolute earnings announcement returns than noncyclical sectors such as consumer staples. The healthcare sector is typically a noncyclical sector, but life science and biotechnology companies within the healthcare sector tend to have volatile earnings due to the unpredictability of scientific research.

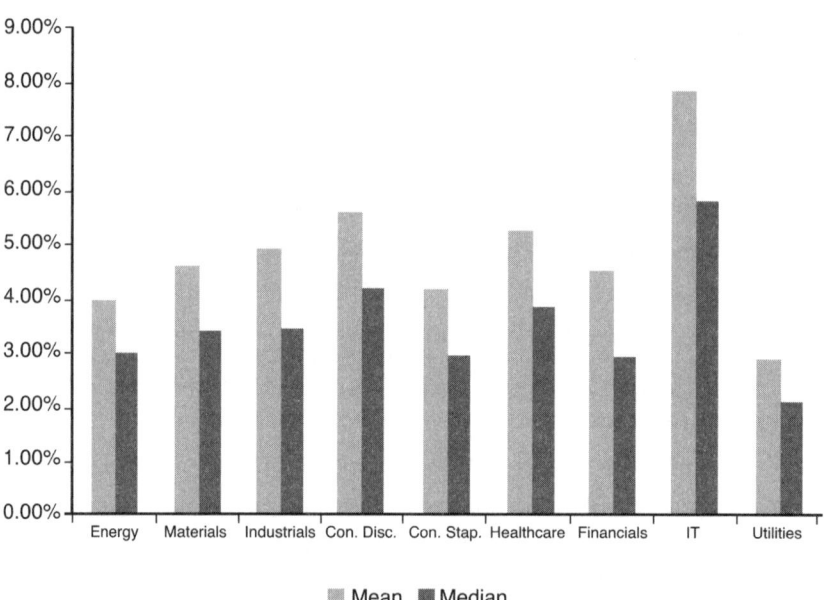

Figure 14.1 Absolute earnings announcement returns by sectors.

Implied Volatility by Sector

Implied volatility before earnings announcements for the nine sectors is shown in Figure 14.2. Detailed data are provided in Table A14.2 in the "Appendix" section. The graph reveals that the market acknowledges variances in earnings volatility across sectors. For example, the mean (median) implied volatility was highest for the information technology sector at 70.62% (65.65%), consistent with this sector's highest absolute earnings announcement returns. The consumer staples sector's mean (median) implied volatility was 36.90% (33.39%), which was the lowest among the nine sectors. The utilities sector, which had the lowest absolute earnings announcement returns, had slightly higher implied volatility than the consumer staples sector. The rank of implied volatility for the sectors does not match exactly with the rank of the absolute earnings return volatility, but they are very close. This analysis was performed on an aggregate basis across the 20 years examined. Implied volatility can be quite different across these sectors depending on which year or time period was examined. For instance, the financial sector in aggregate across these years seemed to have relatively low implied volatility, but its implied volatility jumped during the more recent financial crisis.

Performance of Long and Short Straddles around Earnings Announcements by Sector

In the preceding sections, we found that there were significant cross-sectional differences in both absolute earnings announcement returns and implied volatility among the nine sectors. In general, cyclical sectors had more volatile earnings announcement returns and higher implied volatility than noncyclical sectors. We now examine how the performance of the long and short straddle strategies around earnings announcements varies across these different sectors.

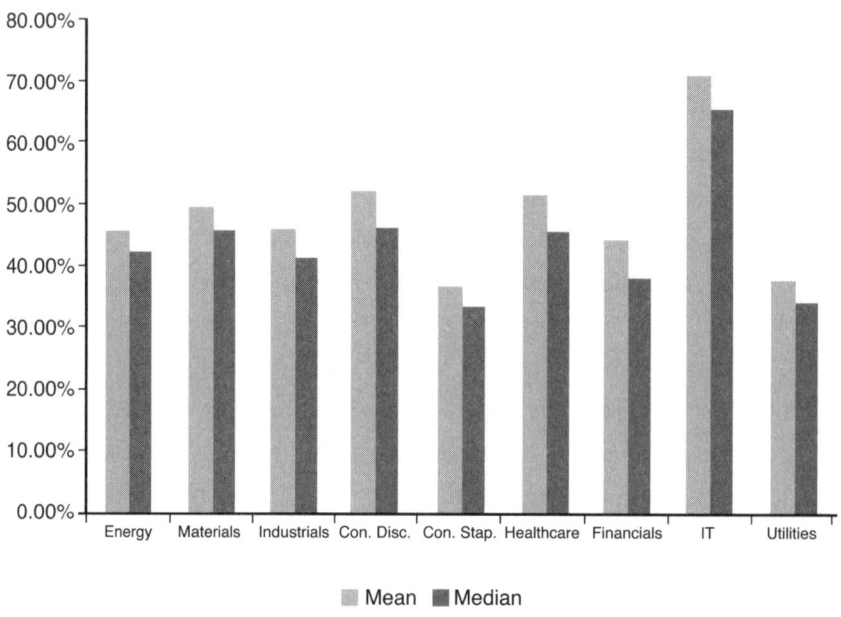

Figure 14.2 Implied volatility by sectors.

The long straddle results are reported in Table 14.1. The conservative 75% rule was assumed for option return calculations. The information technology sector had the highest return of the long straddle strategy (mean return: −2.82%), despite the fact that it had the highest implied volatility. A possible explanation for the finding is that stocks in this sector also had the highest absolute earnings announcement returns. On the contrary, the utilities sector had the lowest return of the long straddle strategy (mean return: −9.79%), despite its lowest implied volatility, because there are few surprises in utilities companies' earnings announcements.

However, this is not to say that investors who want to buy straddles should avoid sectors with small absolute earnings announcement returns. The consumer staples sector had the second-smallest absolute earnings announcement returns among the sectors, but it had the lowest implied volatility. The mean return (–3.07%) of the long straddle for the consumer staples sector was the second highest, trailing only the information technology sector. This was because the consumer staples sector had quite a few surprising announcements, which caused the magnitude of earnings announcement returns to be much higher than anticipated based on the sector's implied volatility. For example, the 3rd Quartile return of the consumer staples sector, 8.31%, was much higher than that of any other sector.

Table 14.1 Performance of Long Straddles by Sector

Sector	Obs.	Mean	Minimum	1st Quartile	Median	3rd Quartile	Maximum
Energy	1669	–4.28%	–52.80%	–16.75%	–8.96%	1.95%	142.91%
Materials	946	–5.30%	–53.17%	–17.72%	–10.07%	1.14%	107.45%
Industrials	1648	–4.34%	–74.80%	–19.63%	–10.21%	4.89%	211.83%
Con. Disc.	2501	–4.13%	–67.16%	–20.92%	–10.00%	5.03%	290.99%
Con. Stap.	739	–3.07%	–62.77%	–21.57%	–10.03%	8.31%	198.77%
Healthcare	2670	–3.49%	–69.90%	–20.00%	–9.13%	4.84%	207.31%
Financials	1686	–3.47%	–72.15%	–17.82%	–8.57%	4.85%	253.93%
IT	4910	–2.82%	–75.95%	–18.95%	–8.11%	5.95%	278.86%
Utilities	133	–9.79%	–58.67%	–20.15%	–11.66%	–3.09%	184.54%

Performance of short straddles by sector is reported in Table 14.2. The median returns for all sectors were positive, revealing that selling straddles is a generally more profitable strategy than buying straddles, perhaps because implied volatility regularly exceeds realized volatility. The utilities sector had the highest return (mean return: 1.20%) because its earnings announcements were so uneventful that even its low implied volatility was too high for the risk that option sellers bear. The information technology sector had one of the worst short straddle performances despite having the highest implied volatility among all sectors. The consumer staples sector had the lowest average return (–5.04%) for the short straddle because there were quite a few surprising announcements that generated large negative returns. Its median return for the strategy, 2.21%, was ranked in the middle of the nine sectors, but its 1st Quartile return, –17.42%, was the lowest of all sectors.

Table 14.2 Performance of Short Straddles by Sector

Sector	Obs.	Mean	Minimum	1st Quartile	Median	3rd Quartile	Maximum
Energy	1669	–2.98%	–157.41%	–9.31%	1.67%	10.06%	45.81%
Materials	946	–2.14%	–121.56%	–9.38%	3.28%	11.42%	48.19%
Industrials	1648	–3.38%	–231.23%	–12.99%	3.06%	12.99%	71.01%
Con. Disc.	2501	–3.63%	–314.54%	–13.13%	2.45%	14.24%	63.08%
Con. Stap.	739	–5.04%	–224.44%	–17.42%	2.21%	14.73%	55.87%
Healthcare	2670	–4.19%	–216.95%	–13.20%	1.78%	13.13%	65.43%
Financials	1686	–4.25%	–269.18%	–12.40%	1.08%	11.19%	67.97%
IT	4910	–4.32%	–315.38%	–13.62%	1.39%	12.80%	72.40%
Utilities	133	1.20%	–212.18%	–5.81%	3.05%	12.67%	45.58%

Figure 14.3 shows the hit ratios of the long and short straddles by sector. Detailed data are provided in Table A14.3 in the "Appendix" section. Hit ratios of the short straddle were substantially higher than those of the long straddle for all sectors. Hit ratios of the short straddle were above 50% for all sectors, whereas the hit ratios of the long straddle were mostly below 30%. The sharpest contrast was in the utilities sector, which had the highest hit ratio of the short straddles, approaching 60%, and the lowest hit ratio of the long straddles, only 20%. The consumer staples and information technology sectors offered better opportunities for the long straddle strategy, whereas the utilities, materials, and industrials sectors were more suitable for the short straddle strategy.

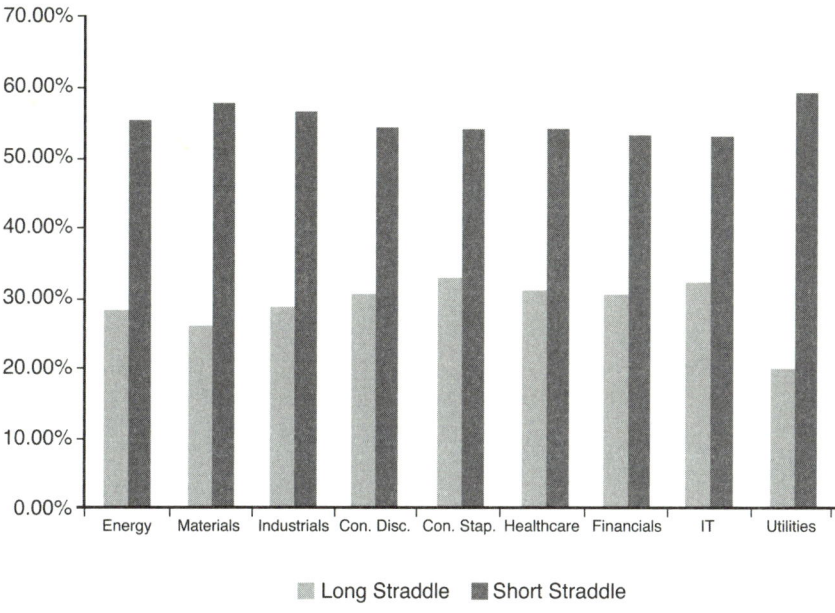

Figure 14.3 Hit ratios of long and short straddles by sector.

The Takeaway

Industry membership is a key characteristic of stocks and options. It not only determines the business and regulatory environment a company operates in, but also affects a stock's performance through basket trading (e.g., passive mutual funds and exchange-traded funds trade stocks in the same industry simultaneously). The information technology sector (including telecom) and the consumer discretionary sector tended to have larger absolute earnings announcement returns than other sectors, perhaps because these sectors were very sensitive to economic growth. Accordingly, implied volatility was highest for the information technology sector, followed by the consumer discretionary sector. On the other hand, the utilities sector and the consumer staples sector exhibited the least volatile earnings announcement returns and lowest implied volatility, consistent with the defensive nature of these sectors.

Long straddles had the best performance for the information technology sector, in spite of the sector's highest implied volatility. Short straddles had the best performance for the utilities sector even though this sector had the lowest implied volatility. These results show that industry membership is another useful signal for security selection.

Endnote

1. There are many ways to classify industries. For example, SIC (Standard Industry Classification) was established by the U.S. government in 1937. It is still used by the SEC and many researchers today.

Appendix

Table A14.1 Absolute Earnings Announcement Returns by Sector

GICS	Obs.	Mean	Minimum	1st Quartile	Median	3rd Quartile	Maximum
Energy	1669	3.96%	0.00%	1.32%	3.05%	5.49%	23.33%
Materials	946	4.58%	0.00%	1.51%	3.45%	6.20%	26.69%
Industrials	1648	4.90%	0.00%	1.64%	3.48%	6.59%	34.84%
Con. Disc.	2501	5.62%	0.00%	1.96%	4.22%	7.81%	48.79%
Con. Stap.	739	4.17%	0.00%	1.37%	3.00%	5.97%	30.33%
Healthcare	2670	5.27%	0.00%	1.83%	3.90%	7.07%	57.55%
Financials	1686	4.49%	0.00%	1.43%	2.98%	5.73%	53.04%
IT	4910	7.80%	0.00%	2.63%	5.83%	10.70%	63.76%
Utilities	133	2.91%	0.00%	1.15%	2.09%	3.47%	18.16%

Table A14.2 Implied Volatility by Sector

GICS	Obs.	Mean	Minimum	1st Quartile	Median	3rd Quartile	Maximum
Energy	1669	45.78%	15.61%	34.05%	42.42%	53.04%	145.67%
Materials	946	49.36%	17.31%	36.17%	45.61%	57.28%	186.73%
Industrials	1648	45.81%	12.56%	30.26%	41.44%	56.09%	162.53%
Con. Disc.	2501	51.92%	16.68%	36.74%	46.22%	62.46%	199.06%
Con. Stap.	739	36.90%	12.92%	24.61%	33.39%	44.04%	134.89%
Healthcare	2670	51.61%	11.53%	34.26%	45.65%	62.38%	321.32%
Financials	1686	44.17%	12.47%	26.71%	37.91%	52.24%	185.12%
IT	4910	70.62%	13.38%	48.03%	65.65%	87.35%	245.55%
Utilities	133	37.47%	11.70%	23.91%	34.13%	46.12%	124.32%

Table A14.3 Hit Ratios of Long and Short Straddles by Sector

GICS	Obs.	Long Straddle	Short Straddle
Energy	1669	27.98%	55.12%
Materials	946	26.00%	57.82%
Industrials	1648	28.88%	57.16%
Con. Disc.	2501	30.31%	54.50%
Con. Stap.	739	33.15%	54.40%
Healthcare	2670	31.16%	54.23%
Financials	1686	30.60%	52.85%
IT	4910	32.02%	53.14%
Utilities	133	20.30%	59.40%

15

Enhanced Strategies

In the preceding five chapters, we analyzed the impact of five factors on the performance of long and short straddles and strangles around earnings announcements: implied volatility, historical absolute earnings announcement returns, market capitalization, valuation, and industry membership. The analyses show that among the five factors, implied volatility and market capitalization have the most significant impact on the long and short straddles/strangles. Both factors are negatively related to the performance of long straddles/strangles, and positively related to performance of short straddles/strangles. Volatility buyers do better by focusing on low implied volatility options and options of small-cap stocks, whereas volatility sellers benefit from focusing on high implied volatility options and options of large-cap stocks. The other three factors are also useful for improving options traders' security selection, but to a lesser extent. Options of stocks with large historical absolute earnings announcement returns and high valuation ratios are good candidates for long straddles/strangles, and small historical absolute earnings announcement returns and low valuation ratios are characteristics in stocks favoring straddle/strangle sellers. Historically, stocks in the information technology and consumer discretionary sectors were good candidates for straddle/strangle buying.

So far, the analyses were performed for each factor individually. In this chapter, we design and test volatility strategies that utilize these factors jointly or simultaneously. Our analysis begins with an enhanced volatility strategy that takes into account the two most important factors: implied volatility and market capitalization. Next, we show how the other three factors can further improve the performance of the volatility trade.

Enhancing the Volatility Strategy: A Two-Factor Model

We now analyze how to apply implied volatility before earnings announcements and stocks' market capitalization to improve the performance of long and short straddles around earnings announcements. The sample included only stocks with options that met specific liquidity requirements: (1) the bid-ask spread of the straddle was smaller than 10% of the mid-price and (2) the bid price was greater than $0.60. Stocks without market capitalization data or options without implied volatility information were removed. The final sample had 13,461 observations.

To use the information on implied volatility and market capitalization simultaneously, we performed an *independent double-sort*. First, we sorted all straddles into three equal-size portfolios (terciles) by implied volatility one day before earnings announcements. The three portfolios are termed high, medium, and low implied volatility. Next, we sorted the same straddles into terciles by market capitalization. The portfolios are called large-, mid-, and small-cap portfolios. After this double-sorting procedure, each straddle was assigned to one of the nine (three-by-three) groups.[1]

Long Straddles

The results of the long straddles are summarized in Table 15.1. We report mean and median returns of long straddles for each of the nine portfolios.

Table 15.1 Long Straddles Enhanced by Implied Volatility and Market Capitalization

			Implied Volatility		
			Low	*Medium*	*High*
Market Cap	*Small*	Mean	1.28%	−2.17%	−3.88%
		Median	−6.12%	−8.59%	−8.26%
		Obs.	462	1459	2566
	Mid	Mean	−1.12%	−3.64%	−6.56%
		Median	−9.73%	−9.89%	−9.57%
		Obs.	1432	1736	1319
	Large	Mean	−3.30%	−7.04%	−6.41%
		Median	−9.91%	−10.54%	−10.63%
		Obs.	2593	1292	602

Three interesting observations emerge from the data. First, the number of observations does not distribute evenly across the nine buckets because implied volatility and market cap were sorted independently. Small-cap stocks tended to have high implied volatility (the upper-right-corner group had 2,566 observations), whereas large-cap stocks tended to have low implied volatility (the bottom-left-corner group had 2,593 observations). These two groups represented a disproportionately large number of observations. The two portfolios of greatest interest to us, small-cap/low implied volatility (the upper-left-corner group) and large-cap/high implied volatility (the bottom-right-corner group), had only 1,064 observations when combined together.

Second, our results for implied volatility (Chapter 10, "Implied Volatility") held strongly even after controlling for market-cap information. For instance, whether small-cap, mid-cap, or large-cap stocks were tested, long straddles always had higher mean and median returns for low-implied-volatility groups than for high-implied-volatility groups.[2] Take large-cap stocks as an example. Among all large-cap stocks, the long straddles had a mean (median) return of −3.30% (−9.91%) for the low-implied-volatility options, and the mean (median) return of the long straddles for high-implied-volatility options was –6.41% (–10.63%). Similarly, our results for market-cap (Chapter 12, "Market Capitalization") also held after controlling for implied volatility: Given any implied volatility level, the long straddles had a higher average return for the small-cap stocks than for the large-cap stocks.

Third and most important, low-implied-volatility options of small-cap stocks had the best long straddle performance. The average return of long straddles for this group was positive (1.28%), whereas for all the other eight groups it was negative. The 1.28% return was economically significant because it was achieved in two days. The post-transaction cost return should have been lower, but the return is attractive even after a 50% haircut. The median return for this group was still negative (–6.12%), albeit better than the median return for other groups. The hit ratio for this group was 35%, which was low but still the highest among all nine groups. These results point out that the long straddle strategy was generally unprofitable. Its success depended on capturing the infrequent large, unexpected price spikes. Such opportunities might be more easily spotted in small-cap, low-implied-volatility options.

Short Straddles

Table 15.2 shows the results for the short straddle strategy. The results are a mirror image of those for the long straddle strategy. The short straddles performed better for high-implied-volatility options, regardless of market-cap levels. Similarly, short straddles performed better for large-cap stocks independent of the implied volatility levels. From a hit ratio perspective, short straddles were more profitable than long straddles. Median returns of the short straddles were positive for all but two groups, whereas median returns of the long straddles were all negative. The short straddles had the greatest success with large-cap, high-implied-volatility options (the bottom-left-corner group). Shorting these straddles generated 1.11% average return in two days and the median return was 5.73%. The most successful group with long straddles, the small-cap/low-implied-volatility group, had the worst short straddle performance. The average return was –11.09% and the median return was –2.94% for this group. The hit ratio for the large-cap/high-implied-volatility group was 62%, whereas for the small-cap/low-implied-volatility group it was 44%.

Table 15.2 Short Straddles Enhanced by Implied Volatility and Market Capitalization

			Implied Volatility		
			Low	*Medium*	*High*
Market Cap	*Small*	Mean	–11.09%	–6.60%	–4.11%
		Median	–2.94%	0.41%	0.60%
		Obs.	462	1459	2566
	Mid	Mean	–7.30%	–3.77%	0.00%
		Median	1.60%	2.67%	3.35%
		Obs.	1432	1736	1319
	Large	Mean	–3.75%	–4.11%	1.11%
		Median	3.01%	0.60%	5.73%
		Obs.	2593	1292	602

Further Enhancement

The analysis in the preceding section suggests that volatility buyers should look for candidates in small-cap/low-implied-volatility options, and volatility sellers should focus on large-cap/high-implied-volatility options. This section examines whether we can further improve the performance of the enhanced strategies by incorporating information from the other three factors. Because only a small number of straddles passed the strict selection process of the enhanced strategies (462 for the long straddle and 602 for the short straddle), applying the other three factors simultaneously would significantly reduce the already small sample. Thus, the three factors were applied one at a time. An advantage of this approach is that the effect of each additional factor on performance is more readily observed.

Only the small-cap/low-implied-volatility and large-cap/high-implied-volatility groups were studied in this section. (Because the purpose of this section is to illustrate how additional factors can help improve enhanced strategies, it is natural to start with the enhanced strategies.)

Historical Absolute Earnings Announcement Returns

We first analyze how historical absolute earnings announcement returns helps improve the performance of the enhanced long straddle strategy. The small-cap/low-implied-volatility group was divided into two subgroups based on whether historical absolute earnings announcement returns were greater than 5%. Five percent was picked as the cutoff point because it is roughly the median value of all observations. Table 15.3 shows the results.

Table 15.3 Improve Enhanced Long Straddles with Historical Absolute Earnings Announcement Returns

	Historical Absolute Earnings Announcement Returns	
	< 5%	≥ 5%
Mean	0.50%	2.77%
Median	–6.68%	–5.41%
Obs.	304	158
Hit Ratio	32%	41%

Within small-cap/low-implied-volatility options, the long straddle had a much higher return when applied to those with large historical absolute earnings announcement returns. For this subgroup, the average long straddle return was 2.77%, more than double the 1.28% return for the whole group. The median return was also higher for this subgroup, as was the hit ratio. Thus, options traders can significantly improve long straddle performance by focusing on small-cap/low-implied-volatility options whose past earnings announcement returns were volatile.

The same approach was applied to the enhanced short straddle strategy by dividing the large-cap/high-implied-volatility group into two subgroups based on historical absolute earnings announcement returns. The results are presented in Table 15.4. Performance of the large historical absolute earnings announcement returns subgroup was marginally better than the other subgroup, demonstrating that past earnings announcement returns were not particularly useful in improving the enhanced short straddle strategy.

Table 15.4 Improved Enhanced Short Straddles: Historical Absolute Earnings Announcement Returns

	Historical Absolute Earnings Announcement Returns	
	< 5%	≥ 5%
Mean	1.02%	1.17%
Median	5.56%	5.91%
Obs.	237	365
Hit Ratio	59%	63%

Valuation

In Chapter 13, "Valuation," three valuation ratios, P/B, P/E, and P/S, were analyzed. We select the P/E ratio for this analysis because it is least influenced by industry membership. We start with the enhanced long straddle strategy. The small-cap/low-implied-volatility group was divided into two subgroups based on whether the P/E ratio was greater than 15. Fifteen was selected as the cutoff point because it was roughly the median value of all observations. Table 15.5 shows the results.

Table 15.5 Improved Enhanced Long Straddles: P/E

	P/E	
	< 15	≥ 15
Mean	−2.12%	4.95%
Median	−8.24%	−5.08%
Obs.	240	222
Hit Ratio	30%	40%

Long straddle performance for the high-P/E subgroup was 4.95%, almost quadrupling the 1.28% return for the whole group. In fact, the low-P/E subgroup had a negative average return. The median return was also higher for the high-P/E subgroup, as was the hit ratio. These results were consistent with the findings in Chapter 13 that high-valuation stocks (so-called glamour stocks) tended to have more volatile earnings announcement returns.

We then examine whether the P/E ratio helps improve the performance of the enhanced short straddle strategy. We divided the large-cap/high-implied-volatility group into two subgroups based on the P/E ratio. The results are presented in Table 15.6. Shorting straddles was much more profitable for low-P/E stocks than for high-P/E stocks. The average return for the low-P/E subgroup was 3.45%, more than triple the 1.11% return for the whole group. In fact, the high-P/E subgroup had a negative average return. Both the median return and the hit ratio were much higher for the low-P/E subgroup as well.

Table 15.6 Improved Enhanced Short Straddles: P/E

	P/E	
	< 15	< 15
Mean	3.45%	−1.07%
Median	7.47%	3.97%
Obs.	291	311
Hit Ratio	65%	58%

Industry Membership

Industry membership might help improve the performance of the enhanced volatility strategies as well. We divided the small-cap/low-implied-volatility group into two subgroups based on industry membership. Stocks belonging to the information technology (IT) or consumer discretionary (Con. Disc.) sectors formed one subgroup, and the remaining stocks formed the other. IT and Con. Disc. sectors were chosen because stocks in these two sectors had the most volatile earnings announcement returns. Also, there was evidence that the long straddles were more profitable for the two sectors, especially for IT. Table 15.7 shows the impact of industry membership on performance of the enhanced long straddle strategy.

Table 15.7 Improved Enhanced Long Straddles: Industry Membership

	Industry Membership	
	IT & Con. Disc.	*Others*
Mean	3.67%	−0.23%
Median	−4.91%	−7.24%
Obs.	178	284
Hit Ratio	39%	33%

We found that the long straddle performance for the IT and Con. Disc. subgroup was 3.67%, almost tripling the 1.28% return for the whole group. The Others subgroup had a small negative average return (−0.23%). The median return and hit ratio were also higher for the IT and Con. Disc. subgroup.

The same analysis was performed on the enhanced short straddle strategy. The large-cap/high-implied-volatility options were divided into two subgroups based on industry membership. Results are presented in Table 15.8. Shorting straddles was again more profitable for the IT and Con. Disc. subgroup. The average short straddle return for the IT and Con. Disc. subgroup was 2.49%, more than double the 1.11% return for the whole group. The Others subgroup had a negative average return. Both median return and hit ratio were much higher for the IT and Con. Disc. subgroup as well.

Table 15.8 Improved Enhanced Short Straddles: Industry Membership

	Industry Membership	
	IT & Con. Disc.	Others
Mean	2.49%	−0.63%
Median	6.74%	4.00%
Obs.	336	266
Hit Ratio	63%	60%

The Takeaway

Options traders can significantly improve performance of the long and short volatility trades around earnings announcement returns by applying systematic security selection. In particular, we show that better security selection can be achieved by using the five simple factors analyzed in previous chapters.

Although the average returns of unconditional long or short straddles were both negative, we develop a two-factor model that helps identify straddles for which a long or short strategy generates positive average returns. Specifically, long straddles of small-cap/low-implied-volatility options and short straddles of large-cap/high-implied-volatility options had positive average returns above 1% in two days. These were big improvements when compared to the −3.68% average long straddle return (Chapter 6, "Long Volatility Trades") and the −3.83% average short straddle return (Chapter 7, "Short Volatility Trades").

Combining the additional three factors greatly improves performance of the enhanced strategies. In particular, long straddle performance is much higher if options traders restrict their positions to stocks with volatile historical earnings announcement returns, high valuation, or membership in the information technology or consumer discretionary sectors. For straddle sellers, higher returns are achieved by focusing on stocks with low valuation or membership in the information technology or consumer discretionary sectors.

Endnotes

1. Careful readers may wonder why we don't adopt the same classification criteria we used in previous chapters. Specifically, we classify all straddles into six implied volatility groups (Chapter 10) and five market-cap groups (Chapter 12). We actually tested the double-sort strategy with the original classification criteria and got even stronger results. However, because the original classifications are more granular, only a very small group of options passed the selection process. To increase the likelihood of generalizing these results to other scenarios, the current three-by-three classification scheme was adopted.

2. The only exception was the mid-cap stocks for which the median return of the long straddle was slightly lower for the low-implied-volatility group than for the high-implied-volatility group (−9.73% versus −9.57%), but the mean return was much higher for the low-implied-volatility group than for the high-implied-volatility group (−1.12% versus −6.56%).

Index

Numbers

10-Q financial reports, 4
75% rule bid-ask spreads, impact on performance, 31-36

A

Absolute Bid-Ask Spread, 24
    distribution of, 25-31
        for calls, 25-28
        for puts, 29-31
absolute earnings announcement returns
    implied volatility and, 138-140
    by industry sector, 184-186
    market capitalization and, 162-164
    predicting future returns from historical returns, 151-155
    valuation ratios and, 171-175
ATM (at-the-money), 14-15

B

bearish directional trades, 17-18, 59
    after earnings announcements, 127-130
    further expiration dates, 66-67
    increased holding period, 67-68
    long puts, 59-60
    OTM (out-of-the-money) options, 64-66
    potential profitability analysis, 69-73
    short calls, 61
    time series analysis, 62-63
bid-ask spreads
    Absolute Bid-Ask Spread, 24
    distribution of, 25-31
        for calls, 25-28
        for puts, 29-31
    impact of assumptions on performance, 31-36
    liquidity and, 23
    Percentage Bid-Ask Spread, 24
book value, defined, 170
bullish directional trades, 17-18, 41
    after earnings announcements, 126-129
    further expiration dates, 48-49
    increased holding period, 49-51
    long calls, baseline case, 42-43
    OTM (out-of-the-money) options, 46-48
    potential profitability analysis, 51-54
    short puts, baseline case, 43-44
    time series analysis, 44-46
buying volatility. *See* **volatility trades**

C

calls
  distribution of bid-ask spreads, 25-28
  impact of bid-ask spread assumptions, 34-35
  long calls
    baseline case, 42-43
    after earnings announcements, 126-127
    further expiration dates, 48-49
    increased holding period, 49-51
    OTM (out-of-the-money) options, 46-48
    potential profitability analysis, 51-54
    time series analysis, 44-46
  short calls
    baseline case, 61
    after earnings announcements, 127-128
    further expiration dates, 66-67
    increased holding period, 67-68
    OTM (out-of-the-money) options, 64-66
    potential profitability analysis, 69-73
    time series analysis, 62-63
change in implied volatility, 144-148
Coca-Cola, absolute earnings announcement returns, 138-139

D

directional trades, 16
  bearish directional trades, 59
    after earnings announcements, 127-128
    further expiration dates, 66-67
    increased holding period, 67-68
    long puts, 59-60
    OTM (out-of-the-money) options, 64-66
    potential profitability analysis, 69-73
    short calls, 61
    time series analysis, 62-63
  bearish versus bullish trades, 17-18
  bullish directional trades, 41
    after earnings announcements, 126-127
    further expiration dates, 48-49
    increased holding period, 49-51
    long calls, 42-43
    OTM (out-of-the-money) options, 46-48
    potential profitability analysis, 51-54
    short puts, 43-44
    time series analysis, 44-46
  after earnings announcements, 21, 121-123
    bearish directional trades, 127-128
    bullish directional trades, 126-127

E

EARET. *See* earnings announcement returns
earnings, defined, 170
earnings announcement returns
  absolute returns
    implied volatility and, 138-140
    by industry sector, 184-186
    market capitalization and, 162-164
    predicting future returns from historical returns, 151-155
    valuation ratios and, 171-175
  historical returns
    enhanced strategies and, 200-201
    performance of straddles, 156-158
    predicting future returns, 151-155
earnings announcements
  market reactions to, 4-6
  reason for importance, 4
earnings surprises, 7
  longing volatility trades, 18-19
  market reactions to, 8-9
event-driven trading, 3
evolution of implied volatility, 144-148
expiration dates, 15
  bearish directional trades, 66-67
  bullish directional trades, 48-49
  long straddles, 85-86
  long strangles, 86
  short straddles, 100
  short strangles, 101
  volatility trades before earnings announcements, 113-114

F-G

future earnings announcement returns, predicting from historical returns, 151-155
GICS (Global Industry Classification Standard), 184
Google, predicting future returns from historical returns, 151-152

H

historical earnings announcement returns
  enhanced strategies and, 200-201
  performance of straddles, 156-158
  predicting future returns, 151-155
hit ratios for long and short straddles
  by industry sector, 190
  market capitalization and, 166
  valuation ratios and, 179
holding period
  bearish directional trades, 67-68
  bullish directional trades, 49-51
  long straddles, 86-87
  long strangles, 87
  short straddles, 101-102
  short strangles, 102
  volatility trades before earnings announcements, 114-115

I

implied volatility, 137-138. *See also* volatility trades
  absolute earnings announcement returns, 138-140

evolution around earnings
  announcements, 144-148
industry sectors and, 187-188
market capitalization and,
  196-199
performance of straddles,
  141-144
industry sectors, 183-184
  absolute earnings announcement
    returns and, 184-186
  classification system, 184
  implied volatility and, 187-188
  long straddle performance,
    187-188, 203
  short straddle performance,
    190, 204
ITM (in-the-money), 14

L

large-cap stocks, 161-162
leverage of options, 12
liquidity, bid-ask spreads and, 23.
  See also bid-ask spreads
long calls
  baseline case, 42-43
  after earnings announcements,
    126-129
  further expiration dates, 48-49
  increased holding period, 49-51
  OTM (out-of-the-money)
    options, 46-48
  potential profitability analysis,
    51-54
  time series analysis, 44-46
long puts
  baseline case, 59-60
  after earnings announcements,
    127-130
  further expiration dates, 66-67
  increased holding period, 67-68

OTM (out-of-the-money)
  options, 64-66
potential profitability analysis,
  69-73
time series analysis, 62-63
long straddles, 79
  baseline case, 80-81
  further expiration dates, 85-86
  historical earnings
    announcement returns and
    performance, 156-157, 200-201
  hit ratios and valuation, 179
  implied volatility and market
    capitalization, 196-198
  implied volatility and
    performance, 141-143
  increased holding period, 86-87
  by industry sector, 187-188, 203
  market capitalization and,
    165, 166
  potential profitability analysis,
    88-89
  time series analysis, 83-84
  valuation ratios and, 174-176,
    201-202
long strangles, 79
  baseline case, 82
  further expiration dates, 86
  increased holding period, 87
  potential profitability analysis, 90
  time series analysis, 83
longing
  in directional trades, 17
  volatility trades, 18-19

M

market capitalization, 161-162
  absolute earnings announcement
    returns and, 162-164
  implied volatility and, 196-199

long straddle performance, 165-166
short straddle performance, 166
market reactions
  to earnings announcements, 4-6
  to earnings surprises, 8-9
mid-price bid-ask spreads, impact on performance, 31-36

N

near-the-money (NTM), 14-15
negative earnings surprises, 7
  longing volatility trades, 18-19
  market reactions to, 8-9
Netflix, absolute earnings announcement returns, 138-139
noncyclical industries, 183
NTM (near-the-money), 14-15

O

option strategies, classifications of, 16
options
  advantages over stock purchases, 11-13
  parameters
    expiration dates, 15
    strike price, 14-15
    timing of trades, 15-16
OTM (out-of-the-money), 14-15
  bearish directional trades, 64-66
  bullish directional trades, 46-48

P

patterns of implied volatility, 144-148
P/B (price-to-book ratio), 171
  absolute earnings announcement returns and, 171-172
  hit ratios, 179
  long straddle performance, 175
  short straddle performance, 177
P/E (price-to-earnings ratio), 171
  absolute earnings announcement returns and, 172-173
  hit ratios, 179
  long straddle performance, 176, 201-203
  short straddle performance, 178, 202
PEAD (post-earnings-announcement drift), 21, 121-123
  bearish directional trades, 127-130
  bullish directional trades, 126-129
  in stock prices, 123-125
Percentage Bid-Ask Spread, 24
  distribution of, 25-31
    for calls, 25-28
    for puts, 29-31
performance
  impact of bid-ask spread assumptions, 31-36
  of straddles
    historical earnings announcement returns and, 156-158
    implied volatility and, 141-144
    implied volatility and market capitalization, 196-199
    by industry sector, 187-190, 203-204
    market capitalization and, 165-166
    valuation ratios and, 174-178, 201-202

positive earnings surprises, 7
  longing volatility trades, 18-19
  market reactions to, 8-9
post-earnings-announcement drift (PEAD), 21, 121-123
  bearish directional trades, 127-130
  bullish directional trades, 126-129
  in stock prices, 123-125
potential profitability analysis
  bearish directional trades, 69-73
  bullish directional trades, 51-54
  long straddles, 88-89
  long strangles, 90
  short straddles, 102-104
  short strangles, 104
  volatility trades before earnings announcements, 115-116
price-to-book ratio (P/B), 171
  absolute earnings announcement returns and, 171-172
  hit ratios, 179
  long straddle performance, 175
  short straddle performance, 177
price-to-earnings ratio (P/E), 171
  absolute earnings announcement returns and, 172-173
  hit ratios, 179
  long straddle performance, 176, 201-203
  short straddle performance, 178, 202
price-to-sales ratio (P/S), 171
  absolute earnings announcement returns and, 174-175
  hit ratios, 179
  long straddle performance, 176
  short straddle performance, 178

pro-cyclical industries, 183
P/S (price-to-sales ratio), 171
  absolute earnings announcement returns and, 174-175
  hit ratios, 179
  long straddle performance, 176
  short straddle performance, 178
puts
  distribution of bid-ask spreads, 29-31
  impact of bid-ask spread assumptions, 35-36
  long puts
    baseline case, 59-60
    after earnings announcements, 127-128
    further expiration dates, 66-67
    increased holding period, 67-68
    OTM (out-of-the-money) options, 64-66
    potential profitability analysis, 69-73
    time series analysis, 62-63
  short puts
    baseline case, 43-44
    after earnings announcements, 126-127
    further expiration dates, 48-49
    increased holding period, 49-51
    OTM (out-of-the-money) options, 46-48
    potential profitability analysis, 51-54
    time series analysis, 44-46

Q-R

quarterly earnings announcements. *See* earnings announcements
risk management of options, 12-13

S

sales, defined, 170
sectors. *See* industry sectors
75% rule bid-ask spreads, impact on performance, 31-36
short calls
  baseline case, 61
  after earnings announcements, 127-130
  further expiration dates, 66-67
  increased holding period, 67-68
  OTM (out-of-the-money) options, 64-66
  potential profitability analysis, 69-73
  time series analysis, 62-63
short puts
  baseline case, 43-44
  after earnings announcements, 126-129
  further expiration dates, 48-49
  increased holding period, 49-51
  OTM (out-of-the-money) options, 46-48
  potential profitability analysis, 51-54
  time series analysis, 44-46
short straddles, 80
  baseline case, 96-97
  further expiration dates, 100
  historical earnings announcement returns and performance, 156, 201
  hit ratios and valuation, 179
  implied volatility and market capitalization, 198-199
  implied volatility and performance, 142-143
  increased holding period, 101-102
  by industry sector, 190, 204
  market capitalization and, 166
  potential profitability analysis, 102-104
  time series analysis, 98
  valuation ratios and, 177-178, 202
short strangles, 80
  baseline case, 97
  further expiration dates, 101
  increased holding period, 102
  potential profitability analysis, 104
  time series analysis, 99
shorting
  in directional trades, 17-18
  volatility trades, 19-20, 95
small-cap stocks, 161-162
stock prices, PEAD (post-earnings-announcement drift) in, 123-125
stock purchases, advantages of options over, 11-13
straddles, 19. *See also* volatility trades
  historical earnings announcement returns and performance, 156-158, 200-201
  hit ratios and valuation, 179

implied volatility and
performance, 141-144
long straddles, 79
   baseline case, 80-81
   further expiration dates,
     85-86
   implied volatility and
     market capitalization,
     196-198
   increased holding period,
     86-87
   by industry sector, 187-188,
     203
   market capitalization and,
     165-166
   potential profitability
     analysis, 88-89
   time series analysis, 83-84
   valuation ratios and,
     174-176, 201-202
short straddles, 80
   baseline case, 96-97
   further expiration dates, 100
   implied volatility and
     market capitalization,
     198-199
   increased holding period,
     101-102
   by industry sector, 190, 204
   market capitalization
     and, 166
   potential profitability
     analysis, 102-104
   time series analysis, 98
   valuation ratios and,
     177-178, 202

strangles, 19. *See also* volatility trades
   long strangles, 79
     baseline case, 82
     further expiration dates, 86
     increased holding period, 87
     potential profitability
       analysis, 90
     time series analysis, 83
   short strangles, 80
     baseline case, 97
     further expiration dates, 101
     increased holding period,
       102
     potential profitability
       analysis, 104
     time series analysis, 99
strike price, 14-15. *See also* **OTM (out-of-the-money)**

T

10-Q financial reports, 4
time series analysis
   bearish directional trades, 62-63, 129-130
   bullish directional trades, 44-46, 128-129
   long straddles, 83-84
   long strangles, 83
   short straddles, 98
   short strangles, 99
   volatility trades before earnings announcements, 111-112
timing of trades, 15-16
trades
   directional trades, 16
     bearish directional
       trades, 59

INDEX **215**

    bearish versus bullish trades, 17-18
    bullish directional trades, 41 after earnings announcements, 21, 121-123
    timing of, 15-16
    volatility trades, 13, 16
        before earnings announcements, 21, 109-110
        long straddles, 80-81
        long strangles, 82
        longing, 18-19
        short straddles, 96-97
        short strangles, 97
        shorting, 19-20, 95

V

valuation ratios, 169-171
    absolute earnings announcement returns and, 171-175
    long straddle performance, 174-176, 201-202
    short straddle performance, 177-178, 202
volatility collapse, 147
volatility trades, 13, 16
    before earnings announcements, 21, 109-110
        baseline case, 110-111
        further expiration dates, 113-114
        increased holding period, 114-115
        potential profitability analysis, 115-116
        time series analysis, 111-112

long straddles
    baseline case, 80-81
    further expiration dates, 85-86
    implied volatility and market capitalization, 196-198
    increased holding period, 86-87
    by industry sector, 187-188, 203
    market capitalization and, 165, 166
    potential profitability analysis, 88-89
    time series analysis, 83-84
    valuation ratios and, 174-176, 201-202
long strangles
    baseline case, 82
    further expiration dates, 86
    increased holding period, 87
    potential profitability analysis, 90
    time series analysis, 83
longing, 18-19
short straddles
    baseline case, 96-97
    further expiration dates, 100
    implied volatility and market capitalization, 198-199
    increased holding period, 101-102
    by industry sector, 190, 204
    market capitalization and, 166
    potential profitability analysis, 102-104

time series analysis, 98
　　　valuation ratios and,
　　　　177-178, 202
　short strangles
　　　baseline case, 97
　　　further expiration dates, 101
　　　increased holding period,
　　　　102
　　　potential profitability
　　　　analysis, 104
　　　time series analysis, 99
　shorting, 19-20, 95

W

worst-price bid-ask spreads,
　impact on performance, 31-36

In an increasingly competitive world, it is quality of thinking that gives an edge—an idea that opens new doors, a technique that solves a problem, or an insight that simply helps make sense of it all.

We work with leading authors in the various arenas of business and finance to bring cutting-edge thinking and best-learning practices to a global market.

It is our goal to create world-class print publications and electronic products that give readers knowledge and understanding that can then be applied, whether studying or at work.

To find out more about our business products, you can visit us at www.ftpress.com.